Relly Victoria Petrescu &
Florian Ion Petrescu

NORTHROP

2012

Scientific reviewer:

Dr. Veturia CHIROIU

Honorific member of
Technical Sciences Academy of Romania (ASTR)
PhD supervisor in Mechanical Engineering

Copyright

Title book: Northrop

Author book: Relly Victoria Petrescu,
Florian Ion Petrescu

© 2012, Florian Ion PETRESCU

petrescuflorian@yahoo.com

Manufactured and published by:
Books on Demand GmbH, Norderstedt
ISBN 978-3-8482-0932-3

Welcome! A Short Book Description:

The Northrop Grumman (formerly Ryan Aeronautical) RQ-4 Global Hawk (known as Tier II+ during development) is an unmanned aerial vehicle (UAV) used by the United States Air Force and Navy and the German Air Force as a surveillance aircraft.

The Northrop Grumman B-2 Spirit (also known as the Stealth Bomber) is an American strategic bomber, featuring low observable stealth technology designed for penetrating dense anti-aircraft defenses; it is able to deploy both conventional and nuclear weapons. The bomber has a crew of two and can drop up to eighty 500 lb (230 kg)-class JDAM GPS-guided bombs, or sixteen 2,400 lb (1,100 kg) B83 nuclear bombs. The B-2 is the only aircraft that can carry large air-to-surface standoff weapons in a stealth configuration.

The BQM-74 Chukar is a series of aerial target drones produced by Northrop. The Chukar has gone through three major revisions, including the initial MQM-74A Chukar I, the MQM-74C Chukar II, and the BQM-74C Chukar III. They are recoverable, remote controlled, subsonic aerial target, capable of speeds up to Mach 0.86 and altitudes from 30 to 40,000 ft (10 to 12,000 m).

Northrop Grumman Corporation (NYSE: NOC) is an American global aerospace and defense technology company formed by the 1994 purchase of Grumman by Northrop. The company was the fourth-largest defense contractor in the world as of 2010, and the largest builder of naval vessels. Northrop Grumman employs over 75,000 people worldwide. Its 2010 annual revenue is reported at US$34 billion. Northrop Grumman ranks #72 on the 2011 Fortune 500 list of America's largest corporations and ranks in the top ten military-friendly employers. It has its headquarters in Falls Church, Virginia.

Separate sectors, such as Aerospace Systems, produce aircraft for the US and other nations. The B-2 Spirit strategic bomber, the E-8C Joint STARS surveillance aircraft, the RQ-4 Global Hawk, and the T-38 Talon supersonic trainer, are used by the US Air Force. The US Army uses Northrop Grumman's RQ-5 Hunter unmanned air vehicle, which have been in operational use for more than 10 years. The US Navy uses Northrop Grumman-built aerial vehicles such as the BQM-74 Chukar, RQ-4 Global Hawk based BAMS UAS, C-2 Greyhound, E-2 Hawkeye, and the EA-6B Prowler. Northrop Grumman provides major components and assemblies for different aircraft such as F/A-18 Hornet, F/A-18E/F Super Hornet and the EA-18G Growler. Many aircraft, such as the F-5, T-38 Talon, and E-2 Hawkeye are used by other nations.

Northrop Grumman Global Hawk

Northrop Grumman RQ-4 Global Hawk

The Northrop Grumman (formerly Ryan Aeronautical) RQ-4 Global Hawk (known as Tier II+ during development) is an unmanned aerial vehicle (UAV) used by the United States Air Force and Navy and the German Air Force as a surveillance aircraft.

In role and operational design, the Global Hawk is similar to the Lockheed U-2, the venerable 1950s spy plane. It is a theater commander's asset to provide a broad overview and systematic target surveillance. For this purpose, the Global Hawk is able to provide high resolution synthetic aperture radar (SAR) – that can penetrate cloud-cover and sandstorms – and electro-optical/infrared (EO/IR) imagery at long range with long loiter times over target areas. It can survey as much as 40,000 square miles (103,600 square kilometers) of terrain a day.

It is used as a high-altitude platform for surveillance and security. Missions for the Global Hawk cover the spectrum of intelligence collection capability to support forces in worldwide military operations. According to the Air Force, the capabilities of the aircraft allow more precise targeting of weapons and better protection of forces through superior surveillance capabilities.

The Global Hawk costs about US$35 million to procure each aircraft. With development costs included, the unit cost rises to US$218 million.

Initial development

The first seven aircraft were built under the Advanced Concept Technology Demonstration (ACTD) program, sponsored by DARPA, in order to evaluate the design and its capabilities. Due to world circumstances, the capabilities of the aircraft were in high demand, so the prototype aircraft were operated by the U.S. Air Force in the War in Afghanistan.

In an unusual move, the aircraft entered initial low-rate production while still in engineering and manufacturing development. Nine production Block 10 aircraft (sometimes referred to as RQ-4A configuration) were produced, two of which were sold to the US Navy. Two more were sent to Iraq to support operations there. The final Block 10 aircraft was delivered on June 26, 2006.

A maintenance crew prepares a Global Hawk for a test at Beale Air Force Base

In order to increase the aircraft's capabilities, the airframe was redesigned, with the nose section and wings being stretched. The changes, with the designation RQ-4B Block 20, allow the aircraft to carry up to 3,000 pounds of internal payload. These changes were introduced with the first Block 20 aircraft, the 17th Global Hawk produced, which was rolled out in a ceremony on August 25, 2006.

First flight of the Block 20 from the USAF Plant 42 in Palmdale, California to Edwards Air Force Base took place on 1 March 2007. Developmental testing of Block 20 took place in 2008. Future Block 30 and 40 aircraft, similar in size to the Block 20, are scheduled for development from 2008 to 2010. When the Global Hawk was produced it was in a sale plan for more than 5 countries including USA and Germany.

United States Navy version

The United States Navy took delivery of two of the Block 10 aircraft to be used to evaluate maritime surveillance capabilities, designated N-1 (BuNo 166509) and N-2 (BuNo 166510). The initial example was tested in a naval configuration at Edwards Air Force Base for several months, later ferrying to NAS Patuxent River on 28 March 2006 to begin the Global Hawk Maritime Demonstration (GHMD) program. Navy squadron VX-20 was tasked with operating the GHMD system.

The GHMD aircraft flew in the Rim of the Pacific (RIMPAC) exercise for the first time in July 2006. Although RIMPAC operations were in the vicinity of Hawaii, the aircraft was operated from Edwards, requiring flights of approximately 2,500 miles (4,000 km) each way to the operations area. Four flights were performed, resulting in over 24 hours of persistent maritime surveillance coordinated with USS Abraham Lincoln and USS Bonhomme Richard. As a part of the demonstration program, Global Hawk was tasked with maintenance of maritime situational awareness, contact tracking, and imagery support of various exercise operations. The imagery obtained by Global Hawk was transmitted to NAS Patuxent River for processing before being forwarded on to the fleet operations off Hawaii, thus exercising the global nature of this aircraft's operations.

Northrop Grumman entered a version of the RQ-4B in the US Navy's Broad Area Maritime Surveillance (BAMS) UAV contract competition. On 22 April 2008 the announcement was made that the Northrop Grumman RQ-4N had won the bid, with the Navy awarding a contract worth US$1.16 billion. In September 2010, the RQ-4N was officially designated the MQ-4C.

On 11 June 2012 a U.S. Navy RQ-4A Global Hawk crashed near Salisbury, Maryland, during a training flight from Naval Air Station Patuxent River.

Program development cost overruns had put the Global Hawk system at risk of cancellation. Per-unit costs in mid-2006 were 25% over baseline estimates, caused by both the need to correct design deficiencies as well as increase the system's capabilities.

This caused some concerns about a possible congressional termination of the program if its national security benefits could not be justified. However, in June 2006, the Global Hawk program was restructured. Completion of an operational assessment report by the Air Force was delayed from August 2005 to November 2007 due to manufacturing and development delays.

The operational assessment report was released in March 2007 and production of the 54 air vehicles planned has been extended by two years to 2015.

In February 2011, the Air Force reduced its planned buy of RQ-4 Block 40 aircraft from 22 to 11 in a cost-cutting move.

The U.S. Defense Department's Director, Operational Test and Evaluation (DOT&E) found the RQ-4B "not operationally effective" for its mission due to aircraft reliability issues in June 2011.

In June 2011, the Global Hawk was certified by the Secretary of Defense as critical to national security following a breach of the Nunn-McCurdy Amendment. The Secretary stated that: "The Global Hawk is essential to national security; there are no alternatives to Global Hawk which provide acceptable capability at less cost; Global Hawk costs $220M less per year than the U-2 to operate on a comparable mission; the U-2 cannot simultaneously carry the same sensors as the

Global Hawk; and if funding must be reduced, Global Hawk has a higher priority over other programs."

On 26 January 2012, the Pentagon announced plans to end Global Hawk Block 30 procurement as the Block 30 was found to be more expensive to operate than the U-2, and its sensor suite was not as capable as the manned aircraft. Plans to increase the procurement of the Block 40 variant were also announced.

Design

The RQ-4 is powered by an Allison Rolls-Royce AE3007H turbofan engine with 7,050 lbf (31.4 kN) thrust, and carries a payload of 2,000 pounds (900 kilograms). The main fuselage is standard aluminum, semi-monocoque construction, while the wings are made of lightweight, high-strength composite materials.

Integrated system

The Global Hawk UAV system comprises an air vehicle segment consisting of air vehicles with sensor payloads, avionics, and data links; a ground segment consisting of a Launch and Recovery Element (LRE), and a Mission Control Element (MCE) with embedded ground communications equipment; a support element; and trained personnel.

The Integrated Sensor Suite (ISS) is provided by Raytheon and consists of a synthetic aperture radar (SAR), electro-optical (EO), and infrared (IR) sensors. Either the EO or the IR sensors can operate simultaneously with the SAR.

Each of the sensors provides wide area search imagery and a high-resolution spot mode.

The SAR has a ground moving target indicator (GMTI) mode, which can provide a text message providing the moving target's position and velocity. Both SAR and EO/IR imagery are processed on board the aircraft and transmitted to the MCE as individual frames.

The MCE can mosaic these frames into images prior to further dissemination.

Navigation is via inertial navigation with integrated Global Positioning System updates.

Global Hawk is intended to operate autonomously and "untethered" using a satellite data link (either Ku or UHF) for sending sensor data from the aircraft to the MCE.

The common data link can also be used for direct down link of imagery when the

UAV is operating within line-of-sight of users with compatible ground stations.

The ground segment consists of a Mission Control Element (MCE) and Launch and Recovery Element (LRE), provided by Raytheon.

The MCE is used for mission planning, command and control, and image processing and dissemination; an LRE for controlling launch and recovery; and associated ground support equipment. (The LRE provides precision differential global positioning system corrections for navigational accuracy during takeoff and landings, while precision coded GPS supplemented with an inertial navigation system is used during mission execution.) By having separable elements in the ground segment, the MCE and the LRE can operate in geographically separate locations, and the MCE can be deployed with the supported command's primary exploitation site. Both ground segments are contained in military shelters with external antennas for line-of-sight and satellite communications with the air vehicles.

Sensor packages

The Global Hawk carries the Hughes Integrated Surveillance & Reconnaissance (HISAR) sensor system.

HISAR is a lower-cost derivative of the ASARS-2 package that Hughes developed for the Lockheed U-2.

HISAR is also fitted in the US Army's RC-7B Airborne Reconnaissance Low Multifunction (ARLM) manned surveillance aircraft, and is being sold on the international market.

HISAR integrates a SAR-MTI system, along with an optical and an infrared imager. All three sensors are controlled and their outputs filtered by a common processor. The digital sensor data can be transmitted at up to 50 Mbit/s to a ground station in real time, either directly or through a communications satellite link.

The SAR-MTI system operates in the X-band and provides a number of operational modes:

The wide-area MTI mode can detect moving targets within a radius of 62 miles (100 kilometers).

The combined SAR-MTI strip mode provides 20 foot (6 meter) resolution over a swath 23 miles (37 kilometers) wide at ranges from 12.4 to 68 miles (20 to 110 kilometers).

The SAR spot mode can provide 6 foot (1.8 meter) resolution over 3.8 square miles (10 square kilometers), as well as provide a sea-surveillance function.

The visible and infrared imagers share the same gimballed sensor package, and use common optics, providing a telescopic close-up capability.

It can be optionally fitted with an auxiliary SIGINT package. To improve survivability, the Global Hawk is fitted with a Raytheon developed AN/ALR-89 self-protection suite consisting of the AN/AVR-3 Laser Warning System, AN/APR-49 Radar Warning Receiver and a jamming system. An ALE-50 towed decoy also aids in the Global Hawk's deception of enemy air defenses.

In July 2006, the US Air Force began testing segments of the improved Global Hawk Block 30 upgrades in the Benefield Anechoic Facility at Edwards AFB.

This version incorporates an extremely sensitive SIGINT processor known as the Advanced Signals Intelligence Payload.

In September 2006, testing began on a new specialty radar system, the Multi-Platform Radar Technology Insertion Program, or MP-RTIP, on board the Scaled Composites Proteus. Once validated, one Global Hawk will be modified to carry this radar set. Previously, the Air Force was considering a larger variant of the MP-RTIP (known as the Wide-Area Surveillance or WAS sensor) for the canceled E-10 MC2A testbed or E-8 Joint STARS aircraft.

In August 2010, Northrop announced that a new version, Block 40, was about to commence production; it would have a new sensor capabilities, including MP-RTIP radar, emphasising surveillance over reconnaissance.

The Block 40 design also has a modified undercarriage.

Operational history

Air Force Global Hawk flight test evaluations are performed by the 452nd Flight Test Squadron at Edwards AFB. Operational USAF aircraft are flown by the 9th Reconnaissance Wing, 12th Reconnaissance Squadron at Beale Air Force Base.

Global Hawk ATCD prototypes have been used in the War in Afghanistan and in the Iraq War.

Since April 2010, they fly the Northern Route, from Beale AFB over Canada to South-East Asia and back, reducing flight time and improving maintenance. While their data-collection capabilities have been praised, the program did lose three prototype aircraft, more than one quarter of the aircraft used in the wars, being lost.

The crashes were reported to be due to "technical failures or poor maintenance", with a failure rate per hour flown over 100 times higher than the F-16 fighters flown in the same wars.

The manufacturer stated that it was unfair to compare the failure rates of a mature design to that of a prototype aircraft.

Three Global Hawks have been lost in accidents through 2003.

On 11 February 2010, the Global Hawks, deployed in the Central Command AOR accrued 30,000 combat hours and 1,500 plus sorties.

Initial operational capability was declared for the RQ-4 Block 30 in August 2011.

After the 2011 Tōhoku earthquake and tsunami, the aircraft flew 300 hours over the affected areas in Japan. There were also plans to survey the No. 4 reactor at the Fukushima Daiichi Nuclear Power Plant.

On 21 March 2001, aircraft number 982003, the third ACTD aircraft produced, set an official world endurance record for UAVs, at 30 hours, 24 minutes and 1 second, flying from Edwards. During the same flight, it set an absolute altitude record of 19,928 meters (65,381 ft), which was later broken by the NASA Helios Prototype (although the absolute record was broken, the Global Hawk's record still stands in its FAI class category).

On 24 April 2001 a Global Hawk flew non-stop from Edwards in the US to RAAF Base Edinburgh in Australia, making history by being the first pilotless aircraft to cross the Pacific Ocean. The flight took 22 hours, and set a world record for absolute distance flown by a UAV, 13,219.86 kilometers (8,214.44 mi).

NASA

In December 2007, two Global Hawks were transferred from the U.S. Air Force to NASA's Dryden Flight Research Center at Edwards Air Force Base.

Initial research activities beginning in the second quarter of 2009 supported NASA's high-altitude, long-duration Earth science missions.

The three Global Hawks were the first, sixth and seventh aircraft built under the original DARPA Advanced Concept Technology Demonstration program, and were made available to NASA when the Air Force had no further need for them.

Northrop Grumman is an operational partner with NASA and will use the aircraft to demonstrate new technologies and to develop new markets for the aircraft, including possible civilian uses.

According to an article in the March 2010 issue of Scientific American (p. 25-27), the Global Hawk aircraft belonging to NASA were in use for testing purposes as of October 2009, with science missions expected to start in March 2010.

A Global Hawk at NASA's Dryden Flight Research Center

Initial science applications included measurements of the ozone layer and cross-Pacific transport of air pollutants and aerosols.

The author of the Scientific American piece speculates that the aircraft could be used for Antarctic exploration while based in and operated from Chile.

In August and September 2010 one of the two Global Hawks was loaned for NASA's GRIP Mission (Genesis and Rapid Intensification Program), with its long-term on station capabilities and long range it was the best aircraft for the mission to monitor the development of Atlantic basin Hurricanes.

A NASA Global Hawk in flight

It was modified to equip weather sensors including Ku-Band Radar, Lightning sensors and Dropsondes.

It successfully flew into Hurricane Earl off the United States East Coast on September 2.

NASA's Dryden Flight Research Center operates two developmental-model Northrop Grumman Global Hawk unmanned aircraft for high-altitude, long-duration Earth science missions. Acquired from the U.S. Air Force, these autonomously flown aircraft are the first and sixth built under the original Global Hawk Advanced Concept Technology Demonstrator development program sponsored by the Defense Advanced Research Projects Agency.

The ability of the Global Hawk to autonomously fly long distances, remain aloft for extended periods of time and carry large payloads brings a new capability to the science community for measuring, monitoring and observing remote locations of Earth not feasible or practical with piloted aircraft, most other robotic or remotely operated aircraft, or space satellites.

The aircraft's 11,000-nautical-mile range and 32-hour endurance, together with satellite and line-of-site communication links to the ground control station, allow for eventual worldwide operation. Dedicated satellite communication links provide researchers with direct access to their onboard instrument packages during missions. Researchers have the ability to monitor instrument function from the ground control station and evaluate selected data in real time.

Northrop Grumman Aerospace Systems, Rancho Bernardo, Calif., and NASA Dryden created a partnership to operate Global Hawk missions from Dryden. NASA and Northrop Grumman share use of the ground control station, maintenance facilities and the NASA Global Hawk aircraft.

NASA's Science Mission Directorate supports NASA research activities on the aircraft. The Science Mission Directorate has teamed with the National Oceanic and Atmospheric Administration and the Department of Energy to investigate unmanned aircraft systems, specifically the Global Hawk, for Earth observation research.

Initial operational capability for Global Hawk science missions from NASA Dryden was achieved in 2010. A portable ground control station is now operational, making deployments and missions possible worldwide. The Hurricane and Severe Storm Sentinel multi-year study beginning in 2012 will be the first deployment opportunity for two NASA Global Hawks that will operate temporarily from NASA's Wallops Flight Facility in Wallops Island, Va.

The 44-foot-long Global Hawk has a wingspan of more than 116 feet, a height of 15 feet, and a gross takeoff weight of 26,750 pounds, including a 1,500-pound payload capability. A single Rolls-Royce AE3007H turbofan engine powers the aircraft. The distinctive V-tail, engine cover, aft fuselage and wings are constructed primarily of graphite composite materials. The center fuselage is constructed of conventional aluminum, while various fairings and radomes feature fiberglass composite construction.

NASA has an additional Advanced Technology Demonstrator, the seventh Global Hawk built, and two Block 10 aircraft transferred from the U.S. Air Force. These aircraft are being used to provide parts for the flying Global Hawks and could be used for future missions.

This image captures a perspective of NASA's Global Hawk unmanned aircraft from one of the wings. The Global Hawk is sitting at the aircraft hangar of NASA's Wallops Flight Facility in Wallops Island, Va. on Sept. 7, 2012.

NASA Global Hawk Pilots Face Challenges Flying Hurricane Missions

NASA's Hurricane and Severe Storm Sentinel, or HS3, mission will be a complex one for the pilots flying NASA's Global Hawk aircraft from the ground. The mission, set to begin this month, will be the first deployment for the unmanned aircraft away from their regular base of operations at the Dryden Flight Research Center on Edwards Air Force Base, Calif. In addition the pilots will be operating the aircraft from two locations on opposite coasts.

After the upload of specialized science equipment is complete, the two Global Hawks will fly from one coast of the United States to another over sparsely populated areas and open water to reach NASA's Wallops Flight Facility in Virginia.

NASA Wallops was selected as a deployment site because the area of scientific interest is the Atlantic Ocean, especially the eastern Atlantic where hurricanes begin to form. Flights from the U.S. East Coast take less transit time to the target than those from NASA Dryden and allow the aircraft to travel further out over the Atlantic and collect data for a longer period of time.

Waiting at Wallops will be a mobile ground control center, mobile payload operations center and Ku-band satellite dish – all necessary for operation of the high-altitude and long-endurance aircraft. Scientists, maintenance personnel and three pilots will support flights from Wallops.

During takeoff and landing of the Global Hawk, the aircraft must be in line-of-sight communications with the pilot. The pilots deployed to Wallops will manage this activity from the Global Hawk Mobile Operations Facility, handing off operation of the aircraft to Dryden after reaching an altitude of approximately 30,000 feet.

Additional pilots sitting in Dryden's Global Hawk Operations Center will receive the verbal hand-off via telephone, cross check data links with pilots at Wallops, and assume responsibility for the aircraft's operation until the mission is completed when the landing operation transfers back to Wallops. This close coordination alleviates the necessity to deploy a larger number of pilots.

When an unmanned aircraft is in the air, the ground-based pilots maintain continual contact with Federal Aviation Administration air traffic control specialists.

The interesting scenario for HS3 is that the pilots are in California's Mojave Desert, talking with East Coast controllers through a radio located on the aircraft. When flying in oceanic airspace, pilots talk with international controllers over telephone. This communication is vital as air traffic controllers provide the altitude and number of other aircraft sharing the same area of the U.S.'s

National Airspace System and international air space as the NASA aircraft. When the Global Hawk reaches an altitude of between 60,000 and 65,000 feet, there are few aircraft competing for space.

Although the flight path of the Global Hawk is pre-programmed into the aircraft's flight control computers prior to a mission, pilots are able to override the flight plan to accommodate the scientists' requests. The scientists will observe flights from the mobile payload operations facility at Wallops where information will stream onto computer monitors from their instruments. The payload manager at Wallops will send the scientists' request for change in altitude or course to Dryden's mission director in the control room with the pilots at Dryden. The pilots operating the Global Hawk change the flight path by entering a new heading, airspeed or altitude on the primary flight display.

All Global Hawk pilots are rated to fly manned aircraft. The pilots commented that it is possible to become so engaged during a Global Hawk flight that it seems like a flying a manned aircraft. They add that much of the sensory information available to pilots of manned aircraft is missing for the unmanned aircraft pilots. It is not possible to smell the fuel, see the weather and terrain, hear the engine starting, or feel the movement from a ground control center. An unmanned aircraft pilot is dependent upon computers and their displays for updates on the health of the vehicle.

The Global Hawk pilots will have to deal with turbulence in the hurricane flights. Fortunately, the cruise altitude is above most of the unstable air associated with that weather phenomenon. In addition, an instrument measuring turbulence was adapted and will be installed with the science payload.

Global Hawk pilots will be well-prepared for the Hurricane and Severe Storm Sentinel mission. They spend hours planning missions, flying a simulator and have a support team in the "cockpit" consisting of a co-pilot, mission director and control room operator. Many are seasoned from flying this type aircraft for the military. Although their tools are a mouse, keyboard and computer displays, the NASA Global Hawk pilots find their work challenging and are proud of the job they do to support the U.S. science community.

NATO

In 2009, NATO announced that it expects to have a fleet of up to eight Global Hawks by 2012.

The aircraft are to be equipped with MP-RTIP radar systems. NATO has budgeted US$1.4 billion (€1 billion) for the project, and a letter of intent has been signed. NATO signed a contract for five Block 40 Global Hawks in May 2012.

Luftwaffe

The German Air Force (Luftwaffe) has ordered a variant of the RQ-4B equipped with German sensors, dubbed Euro Hawk. It combines a normal RQ-4B airframe with an EADS reconnaissance payload.

The aircraft is based on the Block 20/30/40 RQ-4B, but will be equipped with EADS' SIGINT package to fulfil Germany's desire to replace their aging Dassault-Breguet Atlantique electronic surveillance aircraft.

That sensor package comes in the form of six wing mounted pods, a first for the Global Hawk.

Euro Hawk at the ILA 2012

The Euro Hawk was officially rolled out on October 8, 2009 and first flight took place on June 29, 2010. It underwent several months of flight testing at Edwards Air Force Base before flying to Germany.

On July 21, 2011, the first Euro Hawk arrived in Manching, Germany where it will be equipped with the SIGINT sensor package.

There it is also slated to undergo more testing and pilot training, until the first quarter of 2012, when it will be officially handed over to the Luftwaffe to be stationed with the Reconnaissance Wing 51.

The costs for the initial five aircraft are approx. €430 million for the development, and €430 million for the actual procurement.

Potential operators

Australia considered the purchase of a number of Global Hawk aircraft for maritime and land surveillance.

The Global Hawk was to be assessed against the MQ-9 Mariner in trials in 2007. The Global Hawk aircraft would have operated in conjunction with manned P-8A Poseidon aircraft by 10 and 11 Squadrons of the RAAF.

This combination, or a similar one, was to replace existing AP-3C Orion aircraft in 2018. In the end, the Australian government decided not to proceed with this plan and canceled the order.

Canada has also been a potential customer, looking at the Global Hawk for maritime and land surveillance as either a replacement for its fleet of CP-140 Aurora patrol aircraft or to supplement manned patrols of remote Arctic and maritime environments, before withdrawing from the joint effort in August 2011.

Spain has a similar requirement, and has existing contacts with Northrop Grumman.

Japan has been reported as being interested in the purchase of three aircraft.

South Korea's Defense Acquisition Program Administration (DAPA) had expressed interest in acquiring at least four RQ-4B and support equipment by 2011 to increase the intelligence capabilities of the South Korean military after the return of the Wartime Operational Control from the U.S. to ROK, and allocated approximately US$19 million for evaluation purposes.

There was ongoing debate among government officials on whether to take the US offer of Global Hawks or to press on with their domestic UAV development program.

In September 2011, the US and South Korea talked about deploying the aircraft near its border with North Korea to view North Korea and the North Korea–China border.

In January 2012, DAPA announced that it was not proceeding with the purchase because the price had risen from US$442M to US$899M, far exceeding the budget allocation. DAPA stated that they were now investigating a purchase of either the Global Observer or the Phantom Eye.

The New Zealand Defence Force is keeping a "watching brief" over Global Hawk, which has the range to conduct surveillance in the Southern Ocean around Antarctica, and in the Pacific Islands.

The acquisition process has not moved beyond an expression of interest. Also being looked at are the IAI Heron and the "Kahu", a indigenously developed hand-thrown drone.

The Indian Navy has expressed interest in acquiring six to eight MQ-4C Maritime Surveillance Unmanned Aircraft Systems.

Global Hawk could not benefit of a nuclear reactor engine due to the total cancellation of the USA nuclear power program for aircraft, in 1961, signed by president John Kennedy.

Global Hawk gets to the heart of what makes hurricanes tick

Cutting-edge NASA technology has made this year's NASA Hurricane mission a reality. NASA and other scientists are currently flying a suite of state-of-the-art, autonomously operated instruments that are gathering difficult-to-obtain measurements of wind speeds, precipitation, and cloud structures in and around tropical storms.

"Making these measurements possible is the platform on which the instruments are flying," said Paul Newman, the deputy principal investigator of NASA's Hurricane and Severe Storm Sentinel (HS3), managed by NASA's Goddard Space Flight Center in Greenbelt, Md. HS3 will use NASA's unmanned Global Hawks, which are capable of flying at altitudes greater than 60,000 feet with flight durations of up to 28 hours— capabilities that increase the amount of data scientists can collect. "It's a brand-new way to do science," Newman said.

The month-long HS3 mission, which began in early September, is actually a more robust follow-on to NASA's Genesis and Rapid Intensification Processes (GRIP) experiment that scientists executed in 2010. Often referred to as "GRIP on steroids," HS3 is currently deploying one instrument-laden Global Hawk from the NASA Wallops Flight Facility on Virginia's Eastern Shore to look at the environment of tropical storms. In 2013 and 2014, a second Global Hawk will be added that will focus on getting detailed measurements of the inner core of hurricanes.

Without this new aircraft, developed originally for the U.S. Air Force to gather intelligence and surveillance data, the team says the mission wouldn't be possible.

The Global Hawk's ability to fly for a much longer period of time than manned aircraft will allow it to obtain previously difficult-to-get data. Scientists hope to use that data to gain new insights into how tropical storms form, and more importantly, how they intensify into major Atlantic hurricanes— information that forecasters need to make better storm predictions, save lives, and ultimately prevent costly coastal evacuations if a storm doesn't warrant them.

"Because you can get to Africa from Wallops, we'll be able to study developing systems way out into the Atlantic," Newman explained. "Normal planes, which can fly for no more than about 10 hours, often miss the points where storms intensify," added Gerry Heymsfield, a Goddard scientist who used NASA Research and Development funding to create one of the mission's six instruments, the High-altitude Imaging Wind and Rain Airborne Profiler (HIWRAP). "With the Global Hawks, we have a much higher chance of capturing these events. Furthermore, we can sit on targets for a long time."

Just as important as the aircraft are the new or enhanced instruments designed to gather critical wind, temperature, humidity, and aerosol measurements in the environment surrounding the storm and the rain and wind patterns occurring inside their inner cores, they added. "The instruments bring it all together," Newman said. "We didn't have these instruments 10 years ago."

The Global Hawk currently on deployment at Wallops is known as the "environmental" aircraft because it samples the environment in which hurricanes are embedded. It carries three instruments.

A Goddard-provided laser system called the Cloud Physics Lidar (CPL) is located in the nose. CPL measures cloud structures and aerosols, such as dust, sea salt particles, and smoke particles, by bouncing laser light off these elements. An infrared instrument called the Scanning High-resolution Interferometer Sounder (S-HIS), provided by the University of Wisconsin in Madison, sits in the belly of the aircraft. It measures the vertical profile of temperature and water vapor.

At the tail end is a dropsonde system provided by the National Center for Atmospheric Research and the National Oceanic and Atmospheric Administration. This system consists of 88 paper-towel-roll-sized tubes that are ejected much like a soda can in a vending machine. As the sensor drops, a parachute slows its descent, allowing the sensor to drift down through the storm while measuring winds, temperature, pressure, and humidity.

In 2013 and 2014, working in tandem with its environmental counterpart, will be a second Global Hawk, known as the "over-storm" aircraft. It will sample the internal structure of hurricanes. It, too, will carry three instruments.

Heymsfield's HIWRAP, for example, will be situated in the belly of the Global Hawk and will be responsible for sampling the cores of hurricanes.

Similar to a ground radar system, but pointed downward, HIWRAP measures rain structure and winds, providing a three-dimensional view of these conditions.

Also onboard this craft will be a microwave system called the High-Altitude MMIC Sounding Radiometer (HAMSR), created by NASA's Jet Propulsion Laboratory in Pasadena, Calif.

Located in the aircraft's nose, this instrument uses microwave wavelengths to measure temperature, water vapor, and precipitation from the top of the storm to the surface.

At the other end of the aircraft in the tail section will be the Hurricane Imaging Radiometer (HIRAD) provided by NASA's Marshall Space Flight Center in Huntsville, Ala.

This microwave instrument measures surface wind speeds and rain rates in an unusual way. It collects this data by measuring the amount of "foaminess" in ocean waters. According to Newman, the amount of foaminess is proportional to wind speeds at the surface.

Although all six instruments measure different conditions, they share one important characteristic: all operate autonomously and deliver data to scientists in real-time—another scientific advance. In the past, aircraft instruments, which often required the presence of a scientist to operate them, would record captured data.

Only after the aircraft landed could scientists begin evaluating what they had collected.

With the Global Hawk, however, the data are transmitted to the ground in real-time. Should conditions warrant, the science team can direct the pilot, who flies the aircraft from a computer console on the ground, to change course or tweak the pre-programmed flight path in some way to maximize or improve the data they are gathering. "With the Global

Hawk and these instruments, we can make better decisions," Heymsfield added.

The five-year mission will continue through 2014, at which time the team hopes to have dramatically improved their understanding of how storms intensify. "The insights we get will benefit forecasters," Newman said. "What we hope to do is take this technique and make it part of the operational forecast infrastructure."

The HS3 mission is supported by several NASA facilities including Wallops, Goddard, NASA's Dryden Flight Research Center at Edwards Air Force Base, Calif., Ames Research Center, Moffett Field, Calif.; Marshall Space Flight Center, Huntsville, Ala.; and the Jet Propulsion Laboratory, Pasadena, Calif.

In addition, the mission also involves collaborations with various partners from government agencies and academia.

HS3 is an Earth Venture mission funded by NASA's Science Mission Directorate in Washington.

Earth Venture missions are managed by NASA's Earth System Science Pathfinder Program at NASA's Langley Research Center, Hampton, Va. The HS3 Project itself is managed by the Earth Science Project Office at NASA's Ames Research Center.

Northrop Grumman B-2 Spirit

Northrop Grumman B-2 Spirit

The Northrop Grumman B-2 Spirit (also known as the Stealth Bomber) is an American strategic bomber, featuring low observable stealth technology designed for penetrating dense anti-aircraft defenses; it is able to deploy both conventional and nuclear weapons.

The bomber has a crew of two and can drop up to eighty 500 lb (230 kg)-class JDAM GPS-guided bombs, or sixteen 2,400 lb (1,100 kg) B83 nuclear bombs.

The B-2 is the only aircraft that can carry large air-to-surface standoff weapons in a stealth configuration.

Development originally started under the "Advanced Technology Bomber" (ATB) project during the Carter administration, and its performance was one of the reasons for his cancellation of the B-1 Lancer.

ATB continued during the Reagan administration, but worries about delays in its introduction led to the reinstatement of the B-1 program as well.

Program costs rose throughout development.

Designed and manufactured by Northrop Grumman with assistance from Boeing, the cost of each aircraft averaged US$737 million (in 1997 dollars).

Total procurement costs averaged $929 million per aircraft, which includes spare parts, equipment, retrofitting, and software support.

The total program cost including development, engineering and testing, averaged $2.1 billion per aircraft in 1997.

Because of its considerable capital and operational costs, the project was controversial in the U.S. Congress and among the Joint Chiefs of Staff.

The winding-down of the Cold War in the latter portion of the 1980s dramatically reduced the need for the aircraft, which was designed with the intention of penetrating Soviet airspace and attacking high-value targets.

During the late 1980s and 1990s, Congress slashed initial plans to purchase 132 bombers to 21.

In 2008, a B-2 was destroyed in a crash shortly after takeoff, and the crew ejected safely.

A total of 20 B-2s remain in service with the United States Air Force.

Though originally designed primarily as a nuclear bomber, the B-2 was first used in combat to drop conventional bombs on Serbia during the Kosovo War in 1998, and saw continued use during the wars in Iraq and Afghanistan.

B-2s were also used during the 2011 Libyan civil war.

Origins

In the mid-1970s the search for a new US strategic bomber to replace the Boeing B-52 Stratofortress was underway, to no avail.

First the B-70 and then the B-1A were canceled after only a few of each aircraft were built. The B-70 was intended to fly above and beyond defensive interceptor aircraft, only to find these same attributes made it especially vulnerable to surface-to-air missiles (SAMs).

The B-1 attempted to avoid SAMs by flying close to the ground to use terrain to mask its radar signature, only to face a new generation of interceptors with look-down/shoot-down capabilities that could attack them from above.

By the mid-1970s, it was becoming clear that there was a different way to avoid missiles and intercepts; known today as "stealth".

The concept was to build an aircraft with an airframe that deflected or absorbed radar signals so that little was reflected back to the radar unit.

An aircraft having stealth characteristics would be able to fly nearly undetected and could be attacked only by weapons and systems not relying on radar.

Although such possibilities existed such as human observation, their relatively short detection range allowed most aircraft to fly undetected by defenses, especially at night.

In 1974, DARPA requested information from US aviation firms about the largest radar cross-section of an aircraft that would remain effectively invisible to radars.

Initially, Northrop and McDonnell Douglas were selected for further development.

Lockheed had experience in this field due to developing the Lockheed A-12 and SR-71, which included a number of stealthy features, notably its canted vertical stabilizers, the use of composite materials in key locations, and the overall surface finish in radar-absorbing paint.

A key improvement was the introduction of computer models used to predict the radar reflections from flat surfaces where collected data drove the design of a "faceted" aircraft.

Development of the first such designs started in 1975 with "the hopeless diamond", a model Lockheed built to test the concept.

Plans were well advanced by the summer of 1975, when DARPA started the Experimental Survivability Testbed (XST) project.

Northrop and Lockheed were awarded contracts in the first round of testing. Lockheed received the sole award for the second test round in April 1976 leading to the Have Blue program.

ATB program

By 1976 these programs progressed to where a long-range strategic stealth bomber appeared viable.

Whereas the B-1 relied on flying around known defense sites and could only change its mission within a limited selection of pre-determined routes, a stealth bomber could fly over the Soviet Union undetected, allowing it to linger and hunt for targets rather than repeatedly entering and leaving the target zone as quickly as possible.

In a nuclear exchange, this strategy permits the aircraft to wait out the initial attacks and find targets that escaped destruction by eliminating the "overkill" that was built into existing war planning.

Also, stealth characteristics negated prior requirements for high speed dash capabilities and extensive electronic warfare suites for protection.

Carter was aware of these developments during 1977, and it appears to have been one of the major reasons the B-1 was canceled.

Further studies were ordered in early 1978, by which point the Have Blue platform had flown and proven the concepts.

During the 1980 presidential election in 1979, Ronald Reagan repeatedly stated that

Carter was weak on defense, and used the B-1 as a prime example.

In return, on 22 August 1980, the Carter administration publicly disclosed that the United States Department of Defense (DoD) was working to develop stealth aircraft, including a bomber.

The B-2's first public display in 1988

The Advanced Technology Bomber (ATB) began in 1979.

Full development of the black project followed, and was funded under the code name "Aurora".

After the evaluations of the companies' proposals, the ATB competition was narrowed to the Northrop / Boeing and Lockheed /

Rockwell teams with each receiving a study contract for further work.

Both teams used flying wing designs. Northrop had prior experience developing the YB-35 and YB-49 flying wing aircraft.

The Northrop design was larger while the Lockheed design included a small tail.

The Northrop/Boeing team's ATB design was selected over the Lockheed/Rockwell design on 20 October 1981.

The Northrop design received the designation B-2 and the name "Spirit".

The bomber's design was changed in the mid-1980s when the mission profile was changed from high-altitude to low-altitude, terrain-following.

The redesign delayed the B-2's first flight by two years and added about US$1 billion to the program's cost.

An estimated US$23 billion was secretly spent for research and development on the B-2 by 1989.

MIT scientists helped assess the mission effectiveness of the aircraft under a five-year classified contract during the 1980s.

Espionage

Both during development and in service, there has been considerable importance placed to the security of the B-2 and its technologies.

Staff working on the B-2 in most, if not all, capacities have to achieve a level of special-access clearance, and undergo extensive background checks carried out by a special branch of the Air Force.

For the manufacturing, a former car plant in Pico Rivera, California was acquired and heavily rebuilt; the plant's employees were sworn to complete secrecy regarding their work. To avoid the possibility of suspicion, components were typically purchased through front companies, military officials would visit out of uniform, and staff members were routinely subjected to polygraph examinations.

The secrecy extended so far that access to nearly all information on the program by both Government Accountability Office (GAO) and virtually all members of Congress itself was severely limited until mid-1980s.

In 1984, a Northrop employee, Thomas Cavanaugh was arrested for attempting to sell classified information to the Soviet Union; the information was taken from Northrop's Pico Rivera, California factory.

Cavanaugh was eventually sentenced to life in prison and released on parole in 2001.

The B-2 was first publicly displayed on 22 November 1988 at Air Force Plant 42, Palmdale, California, where it was assembled. This viewing was heavily restricted, guests were not allowed to see the rear of the B-2. However, Aviation Week editors found that there were no airspace restrictions over the presentation area and took photographs of the aircraft's then-secret planform and suppressed engine exhausts from above, to the USAF's disappointment. The B-2's first public flight was on 17 July 1989 from Palmdale.

The B-2's first public flight in 1989

In October 2005 Noshir Gowadia, a design engineer who worked on the B-2's propulsion system, was arrested for selling B-2 related classified information to foreign countries.

On 9 August 2010 Gowadia was convicted in the United States District Court for the District of Hawaii on 14 of 17 charges against him.

On 24 January 2011, Gowadia was sentenced to 32 years in prison.

Program costs

A procurement of 132 aircraft was planned in the mid-1980s, but was later reduced to 75.

By the early 1990s, the Soviet Union dissolved effectively eliminating the Spirit's primary Cold War mission.

Under budgetary pressures and Congressional opposition, in his 1992 State of the Union Address, President George H.W. Bush announced B-2 production would be limited to 20 aircraft.

In 1996, however, the Clinton administration, though originally committed to ending production of the bombers at 20 aircraft, authorized the conversion of a 21st bomber, a prototype test model, to Block 30 fully operational status at a cost of nearly $500 million.

In 1995, Northrop made a proposal to the USAF to build 20 additional aircraft with a flyaway cost of $566 million each.

The program was the subject of public controversy for its cost to American taxpayers. In 1996, the General Accounting Office (GAO) disclosed that the USAF's B-2 bombers "will be, by far, the most costly bombers to operate on a per aircraft basis", costing over three times as much as the B-1B (US$9.6 million annually) and over four times as much as the B-52H ($US6.8 million annually).

In September 1997, each hour of B-2 flight necessitated 119 hours of maintenance in turn. Comparable maintenance needs for the B-52 and the B-1B are 53 and 60 hours respectively for each hour of flight.

A key reason for this cost is the provision of air-conditioned hangars large enough for the bomber's 172 ft (52.4 m) wingspan, which are needed to maintain the aircraft's stealthy properties, particularly its "low-observable" stealthy skins.

Maintenance costs are about $3.4 million a month for each aircraft.

The total "military construction" cost related to the program was projected to be US$553.6 million in 1997 dollars.

The cost to procure each B-2 was US$737 million in 1997 dollars, based only on a fleet cost of US$15.48 billion.

The procurement cost per aircraft as detailed in GAO reports, which include spare parts and software support, was $929 million per aircraft in 1997 dollars.

The total program cost projected through 2004 was US$44.75 billion in 1997 dollars.

This includes development, procurement, facilities, construction, and spare parts.

The total program cost averaged US$2.13 billion per aircraft.

The B-2 may cost up to $135,000 per flight hour to operate in 2010, which is about twice that of the B-52 and B-1.

In its consideration of the fiscal year 1990 defense budget, the House Armed Services Committee trimmed $800 million from the B-2 research and development budget, while at the same time staving off a motion to end the project.

Opposition in committee and in Congress was mostly broad and bipartisan, with Congressmen Ron Dellums (D-CA), John Kasich (R-OH), and John G. Rowland (R-CT) authorizing the motion to end the project, others in the Senate, such as Jim Exon (D-NE) and John McCain (R-AZ), also opposing the project.

The escalating cost of the B-2 program and evidence of flaws in the aircraft's ability to elude detection by radar, were among factors that drove opposition to continue the program.

At the peak production period specified in 1989, the schedule called for spending US$7 billion to $8 billion per year in 1989 dollars, something Committee Chair Les Aspin (D-WI) said "won't fly financially."

In 1990, the Department of Defense accused Northrop of using faulty components in the flight control system; the threat posed by bird ingestion potentially damaging engine fan blades also required redesigning.

In time, a number of prominent members of Congress began to oppose the program's expansion, including former Democratic presidential nominee John Kerry, who cast votes against the B-2 in 1989, 1991 and 1992 while a US Senator, representing Massachusetts.

By 1992, Republican President George H.W. Bush called for the cancellation of the B-2 and promised to cut military spending by 30% in the wake of the collapse of the Soviet Union.

In May 1995, based on its 1995 Heavy Bomber Force Study, the DOD determined that additional B-2 procurements would exacerbate efforts to develop and implement long term recapitalization plans for the U.S. Air Force bomber force.

In October 1995, former Chief of Staff of the United States Air Force, General Mike Ryan, and former Chairman of the Joint Chiefs of Staff, General John Shalikashvili, strongly recommended against Congressional action to fund the purchase of any additional B-2s, arguing that to do so would require unacceptable cuts in existing conventional and nuclear-capable aircraft, and that the military had greater priorities in spending a limited budget.

Some B-2 advocates argued that procuring twenty additional aircraft would save money because B-2s would be able to deeply penetrate anti-aircraft defenses and use low-cost, short-range attack weapons rather than expensive standoff weapons. However, in 1995, the Congressional Budget Office (CBO), and its Director of National Security Analysis, found that additional B-2s would reduce the cost of expended munitions by less than US$2 billion in 1995 dollars during the first two weeks of a conflict, in which the Air Force predicted bombers would make their greatest contribution; a small fraction of the US$26.8 billion (in 1995 dollars) life cycle cost that the CBO projected an additional 20 B-2s would cost.

In 1997, as Ranking Member of the House Armed Services Committee and National Security Committee, Congressman Ron Dellums (D-CA), a long-time opponent of the bomber, cited five independent studies and offered an amendment to that year's defense authorization bill to cap production of the bombers to the existing 21 aircraft.

The amendment was narrowly defeated. Nonetheless, Congress did not approve funding for the purchase of any additional B-2 bombers.

Further developments

A number of upgrade packages have been applied to the B-2. In July 2008, the B-2's onboard computing architecture was extensively redesigned, it now incorporates a new integrated processing unit (IPU) that communicates with systems throughout the aircraft via a newly-installed fibre optic network.

A new version of the operational flight program software was also developed, legacy code was converted from the JOVIAL programming language used beforehand to C.

Updates were also made to the weapon control systems to enable strikes upon non-static targets, such as moving ground vehicles.

B-2

On 29 December 2008, Air Force officials awarded a US$468 million contract to Northrop Grumman to modernize the B-2 fleet's radars.

Changing the radar's frequency was required as the US Department of Commerce has sold that radio spectrum to another operator.

In July 2009, it was reported that the B-2 had successfully passed a major USAF audit.

In 2010, it was made public that the Air Force Research Laboratory had developed a new material to be used on the part of the wing trailing edge subject to engine exhaust, replacing existing material that quickly degraded.

In July 2010, political analyst Rebecca Grant speculated that when the B-2 becomes unable to reliably penetrate enemy defenses, the Lockheed Martin F-35 Lightning II may take on its strike/interdiction mission, carrying B61 nuclear bomb as a tactical bomber.

However, in March 2012, the Pentagon announced a $2 billion, 10 year-long modernization of the B-2 fleet was to begin, these upgrades would be mainly focused on replacing outdated avionics and equipment.

It was reported in 2011 that the Pentagon was evaluating an unmanned stealth bomber, characterized as a "mini-B-2", as a potential replacement in the near future.

In 2012, Air Force Chief of Staff General Norton Schwartz stated the B-2's 1980s-era stealth would make it less survivable in future contested airspaces, so the USAF is to proceed with the Next-Generation Bomber despite overall budget cuts.

The Next-Generation Bomber was estimated, in 2012, to have an projected overall cost of $55 billion.

Design

The B-2 Spirit was developed to take over the USAF's vital penetration missions, able to travel deep into enemy territory to deploy their ordnance, which could include nuclear weapons.

The B-2 is a flying wing aircraft, meaning it has no fuselage or tail.

The blending of low-observable technologies with high aerodynamic efficiency and large payload gives the B-2 significant advantages over previous bombers.

Low observability provides a greater freedom of action at high altitudes, thus increasing both range and field of view for onboard sensors.

The U.S. Air Force reports its range as approximately 6,000 nautical miles (6,900 mi; 11,000 km).

Side view of a B-2 Spirit

Due to the aircraft's complex flight characteristics and design requirements to maintain very-low visibility to multiple means of detection, both the development and construction of the B-2 required pioneering use of computer-aided design and manufacturing technologies.

Northrop Grumman is the B-2's prime contractor; other contributing subcontractors include Boeing, Raytheon (formerly Hughes Aircraft), G.E. and Vought Aircraft.

The B-2 bears a resemblance to earlier Northrop aircraft, the YB-35 and YB-49 were both flying wing bombers that had been cancelled in development in the early 1950s; allegedly for political reasons.

The B-2 has a crew of two: a pilot in the left seat, and mission commander in the right; the B-2 has provisions for a third crew member if needed. For comparison, the B-1B has a crew of four and the B-52 has a crew of five.

The B-2 is highly automated and, unlike most two-seat aircraft, one crew member can sleep, use a toilet or prepare a hot meal while the other monitors the aircraft; extensive sleep cycle and fatigue research was conducted to improve crew performance on long sorties.

Armaments and equipment

The B-2, in the envisaged Cold War scenario, was to perform deep-penetrating nuclear strike missions, making use of its stealthy capabilities to avoid detection and interception throughout missions.

There are two internal bomb bays in which munitions are stored either on a rotary launcher or two bomb-racks; the carriage of the weapons loadouts internally results in less radar visibility than externally mounting of munitions. Nuclear ordnance includes the B61 and B83 nuclear bombs; the AGM-129 ACM cruise missile was also intended for use on the B-2 platform.

It was decided, in light of the dissolution of the Soviet Union, to equip the B-2 for convention precision attacks as well as for the strategic role of nuclear-strike.

The B-2 features a sophisticated GPS-Aided Targeting System (GATS) that uses the aircraft's APQ-181 synthetic aperture radar to map out targets prior to deployment of GPS-aided bombs (GAMs), later superseded by the Joint Direct Attack Munition (JDAM).

In the B-2's original configuration, up to 16 GAMs or JDAMs could be deployed; an upgrade program in 2004 raised the maximum carriable capacity to 80 JDAMs.

The B-2 has various conventional weapons in its arsenal, able to equip Mark 82 and Mark 84 bombs, CBU-87 Combined Effects Munitions, GATOR mines, and the CBU-97 Sensor Fuzed Weapon.

In July 2009, Northrop Grumman reported the B-2 was compatible with the equipment necessary to deploy the 30,000 lb (14,000 kg) Massive Ordnance Penetrator (MOP), which is intended to attack reinforced bunkers; up to two MOPs could be equipped in the B-2's bomb bays, the B-2 is the only platform compatible with the MOP as of 2012.

As of 2011, the AGM-158 JASSM cruise missile is an upcoming standoff munition to be deployed on the B-2 and other platforms.

A 2000 lb BDU-56 bomb is being loaded onto a bomb bay's rotary launcher, 2004

Systems

In order to make the B-2 more effective than any previous bomber, it has integrated many advanced and modern avionics systems into its design, these have been modified and improved in light of the switch to conventional warfare missions.

The B-2 features the low probability of intercept AN/APQ-181 multi-mode radar, a fully digital navigation system that is integrated with terrain-following radar and Global Positioning System (GPS) guidance, and a Defensive Management System (DMS) to inform the flight crew against possible threats.

The onboard DMS is capable of automatically assessing the detection capabilities of identified threats and indicated targets.

An Air Force maintenance crew services a B-2 at Andersen AFB, Guam, 2004

For safety and fault-detection purposes, an on-board test system is interlinked with the majority of avionics on the B-2 to continuously monitor the performance and status of thousands of components and consumables.

It also provides post-mission servicing instructions for ground crews.

In 2008, many of the standalone distributed computers on board the B-2, including the primary flight management computer, were being replaced by a single integrated system.

In addition to periodic software upgrades and the introduction of new radar-absorbent materials across the fleet, the B-2 has had several major upgrades to its avionics and combat systems.

For battlefield communications, both Link-16 and a high frequency satellite link have been installed, compatibility with various new munitions has been undertaken, and the AN/APQ-181 radar's operational frequency was shifted in order to avoid interference with other operator's equipment.

The upgraded radar features entirely replaced arrays by those of a newer design, the AN/APQ-181 is now an Active Electronically Scanned Array (AESA) radar.

In order to address the inherent flight instability of a flying wing aircraft, the B-2 uses a complex quadruplex computer-controlled fly-by-wire flight control system, that can automatically manipulate flight surfaces and settings without direct pilot inputs in order to maintain aircraft stability.

The flight computer receives information on external conditions such as the aircraft's current air speed and angle of attack via pitot-static sensing plates, as opposed to traditional pitot tubes which would negatively affect the aircraft's stealth capabilities.

The flight actuation system incorporates both hydaulic and electrical servoactuated components, it was designed with a high level of redundancy and fault-diagnostic capabilities.

Northrop had investigated several means of applying directional control that would least infringe on the aircraft's radar profile, eventually settling on a combination of split brake-rudders and differential thrust.

Engine thrust became a key element of the B-2's aerodynamic design process early on; thrust not only affects drag and lift but pitching and rolling motions as well.

Four pairs of control surfaces are located along the wing's trailing edge; while most surfaces are used throughout the aircraft's flight envelope, the inner elevons are normally only in use at slow speeds, such as landing.

To avoid potential contact damage during takeoff and to provide a nose-down pitching attitude, all of the elevons remain drooped during takeoff until a high enough airspeed has been attained.

Stealth

The B-2's low-observable, or "stealth", characteristics enable the safe penetration of sophisticated anti-aircraft defenses and to attack even heavily defended targets.

This stealth comes from a combination of reduced acoustic, infrared, visual and radar signatures to evade the various detection systems that could be used to detect and be used to direct attacks against an aircraft.

The majority of the B-2 is made out of a carbon-graphic composite material that is stronger than steel and lighter than aluminium, perhaps most crucially it also absorbs a significant amount of radar energy. Reportedly, the B-2 Spirit has a radar signature of about 0.1 m^2.

In contrast to the flat surfaces of the earlier F-117 Nighthawk, the B-2 is composed of many curved and rounded surfaces across its exposed airframe to deflect radar beams, additional reduction in its radar signature was achieved by the use of various radar-absorbent materials (RAM) to absorb and neutralise radar beams.

The B-2's clean, low-drag flying wing configuration not only gave it exceptional range, but was also beneficial to reducing its radar profile as well.

Another design feature is the placement of the engines, which are buried within the wing to conceal the engines' fans and minimize thermal visibility of the exhaust.

The original design had tanks for a contrail-inhibiting chemical, but this was replaced in production aircraft by a contrail sensor that alerts the crew as to when they should change altitude.

To reduce optical visibility during daylight operations, the B-2 is painted in an anti-reflective paint.

Innovations such as alternate high-frequency material (AHFM) and automated material application methods were also incorporated into the aircraft to enhance its radar-absorbent properties and lower maintenance requirements.

In early 2004, Northrop Grumman began applying a newly-developed AHFM to operational B-2s.

In order to protect the operational integrity of its sophisticated radar absorbent material and coatings, each B-2 is kept inside a climate-controlled hangar large enough to accommodate its 172-foot (52 m) wingspan.

The B-2's engines are buried within its wing to conceal the engines' fans and minimize their exhaust signature

Operational history

The first operational aircraft, christened Spirit of Missouri, was delivered to Whiteman Air Force Base, Missouri, where the fleet is based, on 17 December 1993. The B-2 reached initial operational capability (IOC) on 1 January 1997.

Depot maintenance for the B-2 is accomplished by U.S. Air Force contractor support and managed at Oklahoma City Air

Logistics Center at Tinker Air Force Base. Originally designed to deliver nuclear weapons, modern usage has shifted towards a flexible role with conventional and nuclear capability.

The B-2's combat debut was in 1999, during the Kosovo War. It was responsible for destroying 33% of selected Serbian bombing targets in the first eight weeks of U.S. involvement in the War.

During this war, B-2s flew non-stop to Kosovo from their home base in Missouri and back.

The B-2 was the first aircraft to deploy GPS satellite-guided JDAM "smart bombs" in combat use in Kosovo.

The use of JDAMs and precision-guided munitions effectively replaced the controversial tactic of carpet-bombing, which had been harshly criticised due to it causing indiscriminate civilian casualties in prior conflicts, such as the 1991 Gulf War.

On 7 May 1999, a B-2 accidentally deployed five JDAMs in a target building that was actually the Chinese Embassy, killing several staff.

The B-2 saw service in Afghanistan, striking ground targets in support of Operation Enduring Freedom. With aerial refueling support, the B-2 flew one of its longest missions to date from Whiteman Air Force Base, Missouri to Afghanistan and back.

A B-2 during aerial refueling which extends its range past 6,000 nautical miles (6,900 mi; 11,000 km) for intercontinental sorties

The B-2's combat use preceded a U.S. Air Force declaration of "full operational capability" in December 2003.

The Pentagon's Operational Test and Evaluation 2003 Annual Report noted that the B-2's serviceability for Fiscal Year 2003 was still inadequate, mainly due to the maintainability of the B-2's low observable coatings.

The evaluation also noted that the Defensive Avionics suite also had shortcomings with "pop-up threats".

During the Iraq War (Operation Iraqi Freedom), B-2s operated from Diego Garcia and an undisclosed "forward operating location".

Other sorties in Iraq have launched from Whiteman AFB. This resulted in missions lasting over 30 hours and one mission of over 50 hours. "Forward operating locations" have been previously designated as Andersen Air Force Base in Guam and RAF Fairford in the UK, where new climate controlled hangars have been constructed.

B-2s have conducted 27 sorties from Whiteman AFB and 22 sorties from a forward operating location, releasing more than 1.5 million pounds of munitions, including 583 JDAM "smart bombs" in 2003.

In response to organisational issues and high-profile mistakes made within the Air Force; all of the B-2s, along with the nuclear-capable B-52s, and the Air Force's intercontinental ballistic missiles (ICBMs) were transferred to the newly-formed Air Force Global Strike Command on 1 February 2010.

In March 2011, B-2s were the first US aircraft into action in Operation Odyssey Dawn, the UN mandated enforcement of the Libyan no-fly zone.

Three B-2s dropped 40 bombs on a Libyan airfield in support of the UN no-fly zone.

In a 1994 live fire exercise near Point Mugu, California, a B-2 drops 47 500 lb (230 kg) class Mark 82 bombs, which is more than half of a B-2's total ordnance payload

The B-2s flew directly from the US mainland, being refuelled by allied tanker aircraft twice on the inbound journey and twice again on the way back across the Atlantic.

In August 2011, The New Yorker reported that prior to the May 2011 US special forces raid into Abbottabad, Pakistan that resulted in the Death of Osama bin Laden, US officials had considered an airstrike by one or more B-2s as an alternative; an airstrike was rejected due to concerns of damage to surrounding civilian buildings.

No operational B-2s have been retired by the Air Force to be put on display. However, B-2s have made periodic appearances on ground display at various air shows.

B-2 test article (s/n AT-1000), the second of two built without engines or instruments for static testing, was placed on display in 2004 at the National Museum of the United States Air Force near Dayton, Ohio.

The test article passed all structural testing requirements before the airframe failed.

The Museum's restoration team spent over a year reassembling the fractured airframe.

The display airframe is marked to resemble The Spirit of Ohio (S/N 82-1070), the B-2 used to test the design's ability to withstand extreme heat and cold. The exhibit features the actual Spirit of Ohio nose wheel door, with its distinctive Fire and Ice artwork, which was painted and signed by the technicians who performed the temperature testing.

The restored test aircraft is on display in the museum's "Cold War Gallery".

A B-2 Spirit on display at the National Museum of the United States Air Force

From 1989 to 2004, the South Dakota Air and Space Museum located on the grounds of Ellsworth Air Force Base displayed the 10-short-ton (9-metric-ton) "Honda-

Stealth", a 60% scale mock-up of a stealthy bomber which had been built by North American Honda in 1988 for an advertising campaign.

Although not an actual replica of a B-2, the mock-up was close enough to the B-2's design to arouse suspicion that Honda had intercepted classified, top secret information, as the B-2 project was still officially classified in 1988.

Honda donated the model to the museum in 1989, on condition that the model be destroyed if it was ever replaced with a different example. In 2005, when the museum received a B-1 Lancer for display (Ellsworth being a B-1 base), the museum destroyed the mock-up.

General characteristics

Crew: 2

Length: 69 ft (21.0 m)

Wingspan: 172 ft (52.4 m)

Height: 17 ft (5.18 m)

Wing area: 5,140 ft² (478 m²)

Empty weight: 158,000 lb (71,700 kg)

Loaded weight: 336,500 lb (152,200 kg)

Max. takeoff weight: 376,000 lb (170,600 kg)

Powerplant: 4 × General Electric F118-GE-100 non-afterburning turbofans, 17,300 lbf (77 kN) each

Fuel Capacity: 167,000 pounds (75,750 kg)

Performance

Maximum speed: Mach 0.95 (550 knots, 630 mph, 1,010 km/h) at 40,000 ft altitude / Mach 0.95 at sea level[118]

Cruise speed: Mach 0.85[58] (487 knots, 560 mph, 900 km/h) at 40,000 ft altitude

Range: 6,000 nmi (11,100 km (6,900 mi))

Service ceiling: 50,000 ft (15,200 m)

Wing loading: 67.3 lb/ft² (329 kg/m²)

Thrust/weight: 0.205

Armament

2 internal bays for 50,000 lb (23,000 kg) of ordnance.[58]

80× 500 lb class bombs (Mk-82) mounted on Bomb Rack Assembly (BRA)

36× 750 lb CBU class bombs on BRA

16× 2000 lb class weapons (Mk-84, JDAM-84, JDAM-109) mounted on Rotary Launcher Assembly (RLA)

16× B61 or B83 nuclear weapons on RLA

A B-2 in formation flight with 8 US Navy McDonnell Douglas F/A-18 Hornets

The U.S. Air Force's B-2 stealth bomber is the flagship of the nation's long-range strike arsenal, and one of the most survivable aircraft in the world. Its unique capabilities, including its stealth characteristics, allow it to penetrate the most sophisticated defenses and hold at risk high value, heavily defended enemy targets.

The B-2 has demonstrated its capabilities in several combat scenarios, most recently during Operation Iraqi Freedom.

The B-2 is the only U.S. aircraft that combines long range, large payload and stealth in a single platform, giving it the ability to project air power anywhere in the world.

It can fly more than 6,000 nautical miles unrefueled and more than 10,000 nautical miles with just one aerial refueling. With its ability to carry more than 20 tons of conventional and nuclear ordnance and deliver it precisely under any weather conditions, the B-2 also has the ability to change the outcome of a conflict with a single mission.

Northrop Grumman, the B-2 prime contractor, leads an industry team that is working with the Air Force to modernize the B-2 to ensure that it remains fully mission capable against evolving worldwide threats.

A range of upgrade programs are improving the B-2's lethality; its ability to collect, process and disseminate battlefield information with joint force commanders or other local first responders worldwide; and its ability to receive updated target information during a mission.

Twenty one aircraft were built in the original B-2 fleet. Today, the fleet consists of 20 aircraft, following the loss, in February 2008, of the Spirit of Kansas, which crashed while taking off from Andersen Air Force Base, Guam, the first such incident in the B-2's 19 years of operation. Since 1989, B-2 aircraft have flown more than 14,000 sorties and accumulated more than 75,000 flying hours without incident, an unprecedented safety record.

Nineteen B-2s are currently based at Whiteman Air Force Base, Mo., home of the 509th Bomb Wing, while one aircraft is assigned to flight testing at Edwards AFB, Calif. to validate software and weapon systems upgrades.

The B-2 Spirit is a multi-role bomber capable of delivering both conventional and nuclear munitions.

A dramatic leap forward in technology, the bomber represents a major milestone in the U.S. bomber modernization program.

The B-2 brings massive firepower to bear, in a short time, anywhere on the globe through previously impenetrable defenses.

Along with the B-52 and B-1B, the B-2 provides the penetrating flexibility and effectiveness inherent in manned bombers. Its low-observable, or "stealth," characteristics give it the unique ability to penetrate an enemy's most sophisticated defenses and threaten its most-valued, and heavily defended, targets. Its capability to penetrate air defenses and threaten effective retaliation provide a strong, effective deterrent and combat force well into the 21st century.

The revolutionary blending of low-observable technologies with high aerodynamic efficiency and large payload gives the B-2 important advantages over existing bombers.

Its low-observability provides it greater freedom of action at high altitudes, thus increasing its range and a better field of view for the aircraft's sensors. Its unrefueled range is approximately 6,000 nautical miles (9,600 kilometers).

The B-2's low observability is derived from a combination of reduced infrared, acoustic, electromagnetic, visual and radar signatures. These signatures make it difficult for the sophisticated defensive systems to detect, track and engage the B-2.

Many aspects of the low-observability process remain classified; however, the B-2's composite materials, special coatings and flying-wing design all contribute to its "stealthiness."

The B-2 has a crew of two pilots, an aircraft commander in the left seat and mission commander in the right, compared to the B-1B's crew of four and the B-52's crew of five.

The first B-2 was publicly displayed on Nov. 22, 1988, when it was rolled out of its hangar at Air Force Plant 42, Palmdale, Calif. Its first flight was July 17, 1989.

The B-2 Combined Test Force, Air Force Flight Test Center, Edwards AFB, Calif., is responsible for flight testing the Engineering, Manufacturing, and Development aircraft as they are produced.

Five of the six developmental aircraft delivered to Edwards are still involved in continuing flight testing.

The first test aircraft is currently kept in flyable storage. Whiteman AFB, Mo., is the B-2's only operational base.

The first aircraft, Spirit of Missouri, was delivered Dec. 17, 1993. Primary maintenance responsibility for the B-2 is divided between Oklahoma City Air Logistics Center at Tinker AFB, Okla. for avionics software (contractor); Ogden Air Logistics Center, Hill AFB, Utah for landing gear and trainers (contractor); and the Northrop-Grumman facility at Air Force Plant 42 at Palmdale for periodic depot maintenance.

The prime contractor, responsible for overall system design and integration, is Northrop Grumman's B-2 Division. Boeing Military Airplanes Co., Vought Aircraft Co., Hughes Radar Systems Group and General Electric Aircraft Engine Group are key members of the aircraft contractor team. Another major contractor, responsible for aircrew training devices (weapon system trainer and mission trainer) is Hughes Training Inc. (HTI) - Link Division, formerly known as C.A.E. - Link Flight Simulation Corp. Northrop-Grumman and its major subcontractor HTI, excluding Link Division, is responsible for developing and integrating all aircrew and maintenance training programs.

B-2 Spirit at the 2005 Edwards AFB Airshow

It was disappointing when we heard over the radio scanner on Saturday that the B-2 Spirit display had been cancelled because of mechanical problems, especially since I'd heard that the Edwards show is one of the very few places where it's possible to see the B-2 banking at close range.

To be honest, we'd been hearing its engines behind us for quite some time and we could see people working on it, so it didn't come as a total surprise when the cancellation came through.

However, shortly afterwards there was the B-2 taxying out for its performance, and it turns out that the only problem had been a broken motor shaft for the crew entry ladder! In this photo, not only can you see the "stealth bomber", but on the other side of the field in the static display area you can see the F-117 "stealth fighter", which really should be the A-

117 "stealth strike plane", especially now that a true stealth fighter in the form of the F-22 Raptor is in service.

B-2 Spirit at the 2005 Edwards AFB Air Show

Here's the extraordinary beast on its takeoff run; with no vertical tail it looks completely other-worldly, but it actually flies much like any other more conventional aircraft.

This one is called "The Spirit of New York", and is based here at Edwards rather than at Whiteman air force base in Missouri, which is the only operational base for them in the continental United States.

You can see that they've put the Edwards "ED" tail code on the landing gear door, since there's no tail to put it on!

"The Spirit of New York"

The unusual scoops on top of the engine pods are auxiliary air intakes which are needed to get extra air flow into the engines at low speeds.

They're rather similar to the auxiliary intakes on top of Russian fighters, but the purpose is different, the Russians using theirs to reduce the probability of damage from ingesting foreign objects on the runway during takeoff.

This particular aircraft is the only flight test B-2, and it's unusual in another way, too - the stenciling on the undercarriage doors was screwed up and so the letters lean the opposite way to all other B-2s.

The unusual scoops on top of the engine pods are auxiliary air intakes which are needed to get extra air flow into the engines at low speeds

With no tail the stealth bomber relies on the control surfaces along the rear of the wing to minimize side-to-side yawing motion; you can see one of those control surfaces deployed here.

During a mission these control surfaces would make the aircraft more visible to radar, so it's thought that yaw is then eliminated by the onboard computer systems applying differing thrusts from the engines on either side.

The funny looking "beaver tail" at the tail end of the aircraft is called the GLAS or "gust load alleviation surface", an on-board computer uses it to smooth out the ride when sensors at the front of the plane detect vertical gusts.

With no tail the stealth bomber relies on the control surfaces along the rear of the wing to minimize side-to-side yawing motion

The four non-afterburning engines are buried within the wing. Apart from everything else, this makes the aircraft very quiet, it just whispers past you even at low altitude.

The four non-afterburning engines are buried within the wing.

Flying wings are very efficient aerodynamically, with much less drag than ordinary aircraft.

The B-2 likes to get into the air and is a little reluctant to come down, so the crews actually put some effort into forcing the plane on a downward trajectory when landing, much like naval aviators flying onto aircraft carriers.

Flying wings are very efficient aerodynamically, with much less drag than ordinary aircraft

This angle shows off the unusual air intakes, which are mounted far back on top of the wing and have an unusual angled shape, all in order to reduce the radar cross section of the plane.

Jet turbine compressor blades have a nasty tendency to "twinkle" on radar screens as they spin, so the air duct is "S" shaped so the blades aren't visible from any angle.

On the F-117 Nighthawk the compressor blades are hidden by metal mesh at the front of the intakes, but this isn't an ideal solution since it impedes the airflow.

This angle shows off the unusual air intakes, which are mounted far back on top of the wing and have an unusual angled shape, all in order to reduce the radar cross section of the plane

There's no drag chute, but one of the B-2's design criteria was the ability to operate from any airfield useable by a 727 airliner, so the rudders are used as air brakes to slow the aircraft down.

This design feature was also used on Northrop's earlier flying wing bombers, and it's referred to as a "rudderon" or "deceleron" because the same panels which are deflected apart to decelerate the plane are also moved in tandem to act as rudders or ailerons.

There's no drag chute, but one of the B-2's design criteria was the ability to operate from any airfield useable by a 727 airliner, so the rudders are used as air brakes to slow the aircraft down

As the 1960s progressed, the US Air Force was working to find a replacement for the Boeing B-52 Stratofortress.

While still the service's primary nuclear bomber, the aircraft was also in use during the Vietnam War dropping conventional munitions.

With the failure of the XB-70 Valkyrie project, emphasis shifted towards the aircraft that would become the Rockwell B-1 Lancer. As work moved forward on this project in the early 1970s, the Defense Advanced Research Projects Agency (DARPA), began requesting information regarding technologies that could deflect or absorb radar signals.

It was believed that if these technologies could be incorporated into an aircraft, it would be impervious to surface-to-air missiles and other radar-based methods of interception. Covertly approaching the aircraft industry in 1974, DARPA selected McDonnell Douglas and Northrop to push forward developing a "stealth" bomber project.

Also included in the discussions was Lockheed as the company had incorporated stealth features into its SR-71 Blackbird spy plane and was currently working on the stealth fighter project that would produce the F-117 Nighthawk.

By 1976, Lockheed's stealth testing, as part of the Have Blue Project, led to the belief that a large stealth bomber could be created. Additional studies followed in 1978 and the following year the Advanced Technology Bomber (ATB) program was initiated.

A fully black project, ATB received proposals from combined teams at Lockheed-Rockwell and Northrop-Boeing. In creating ATB designs, both teams elected to utilize a flying wing configuration.

On October 20, 1981, the design from Northrop was selected and designated B-2 Spirit.

Flown by a crew of two, Northrop's design was powered by four General Electric F118-GE-100 engines which were situated deep within the B-2's wing to minimize their radar and infrared signatures. The B-2's minimal radar signature (approx. 0.1 square meter) was achieved through the use of a variety of composite materials, special coatings, and the aircraft's shape.

By utilizing a flying wing design, Northrop eliminated many of the leading edges which could make the bomber visible to radar.

Capable of flying approximately 6,900 miles, the B-2 was designed for long duration missions and includes a toilet and small kitchen facility.

As computers control many of the aircraft's systems, only one crew member needs to be on duty at a time, allowing the other to sleep or perform other tasks.

Possessing a large payload, the B-2 can carry up to eighty 500 lb. JDAM GPS-guided bombs or sixteen B83 nuclear bombs.

In addition, it is capable of carrying a variety of standoff weapons such as cruise missiles.

Targeting is aided by the aircraft's APQ-181 radar which can correct GPS errors and increase accuracy.

While a black project, existence of the B-2's development was hinted at by President Jimmy Carter during the 1980 presidential election.

The aircraft was first publically displayed on November 22, 1988 at Air Force Plant 42 in Palmdale, CA, with its first public flight taking place on July 17 of the following year. The B-2 Spirit is a multi-role bomber capable of delivering both conventional and nuclear munitions.

Along with the B-52 and B-1B, the B-2 provides the penetrating flexibility and effectiveness inherent in manned bombers. Its low-observable, or "stealth," characteristics give it the unique ability to penetrate an enemy's most sophisticated defenses and threaten its most valued, and heavily defended, targets.

Its capability to penetrate air defenses and threaten effective retaliation provide an effective deterrent and combat force well into the 21st century.

The blending of low-observable technologies with high aerodynamic efficiency and large payload gives the B-2 important advantages over existing bombers.

Its low-observability provides it greater freedom of action at high altitudes, thus increasing its range and a better field of view for the aircraft's sensors. Its unrefueled range is approximately 6,000 nautical miles (9,600 kilometers).

The B-2's low observability is derived from a combination of reduced infrared, acoustic, electromagnetic, visual and radar signatures. These signatures make it difficult for the sophisticated defensive systems to detect, track and engage the B-2.

Many aspects of the low-observability process remain classified; however, the B-2's composite materials, special coatings and flying-wing design all contribute to its "stealthiness."

The B-2 has a crew of two pilots, an aircraft commander in the left seat and mission commander in the right, compared to the B-1B's crew of four and the B-52's crew of five.

The B-2 is intended to deliver gravity nuclear and conventional weapons, including precision-guided standoff weapons.

An interim, precision-guided bomb capability called Global Positioning System (GPS) Aided Targeting System/GPS Aided Munition (GATS/GAM) is being tested and evaluated.

Future configurations are planned for the B-2 to be capable of carrying and delivering the Joint Direct Attack Munition (JDAM) and Joint Air-to-Surface Standoff Missile.

Northrop T-38 Talon

The Northrop T-38 Talon is a twin-engine supersonic jet trainer. It was the world's first supersonic trainer and is also the most produced. The T-38 remains in service as of 2012 in air forces throughout the world.

The United States Air Force (USAF) is the largest operator of the T-38. In addition to training USAF pilots, the T-38 is used by NASA.

A USAF T-38A Talon from 560th Flying Training Squadron, Randolph Air Force Base Texas, flying over the Texas countryside in 2001

The US Naval Test Pilot School is the principal US Navy operator (other T-38s were previously used as USN aggressor aircraft until replaced by the similar Northrop F-5 Tiger II).

Pilots of other NATO nations fly the T-38 in joint training programs with USAF pilots.

As of 2012, the T-38 has been in service for over 50 years with its original operator (the USAF).

Design and development

The basic airframe was used for the light combat aircraft F-5 Freedom Fighter family. In the 1950s Northrop began studying lightweight and more affordable fighter designs. The company began with its single-engine Northrop N-102 Fang concept. The N-102 was facing weight and cost growth, so the project was canceled and the company N-156 project was begun.

Although the USAF had no need for a small fighter at the time, it became interested in the trainer as a replacement for the T-33 Shooting Star it was then using in that role. The first of three prototypes (designated YT-38) flew on 10 March 1959. The type was quickly adopted and the first production examples were delivered in 1961, officially entering service on 17 March that year, complementing the T-37 primary jet trainer. When production ended in 1972, 1,187 T-38s had been built. Since its introduction, it is estimated that some 50,000 military pilots have trained on this aircraft. The USAF remains one of the few armed flying forces using dedicated supersonic final trainers, as most, such as the US Navy, use high subsonic trainers.

The T-38 is of conventional configuration, with a small, low, long-chord wing, a single vertical stabilizer, and tricycle undercarriage. The aircraft seats a student pilot and instructor in tandem, and has intakes for its two turbojet engines at the wing roots. Its nimble performance has earned it the nickname white rocket. In 1962 the T-38 set absolute time-to-climb records for 3000, 6000, 9000 and 12000 meters, beating the records for those altitudes set by the F-104 in December 1958. (The F-4 beat the T-38's records less than a month later.)

The F-5B and F (which also derive from the N-156) can be distinguished from the T-38 by the wings; the wing of the T-38 meets the fuselage straight and ends square, while the F-5 has leading edge extensions near the wing roots and wingtip launch rails for air to air missiles. Under the paint the T-38 wing is constructed of honeycomb material while the wing of the F-5 family uses conventional skin over underlying support structure.

Most T-38s built were of the T-38A variant, but the USAF also had a small number of aircraft that had been converted for weapons training. These aircraft (designated AT-38B) had been fitted with a gunsight and could carry a gunpod, rockets, or bombs on a centerline pylon. In 2003, 562 T-38s were still operational with the USAF and are currently undergoing structural and avionics programs (T-38C) to extend their service life to 2020. Improvements include the addition of a HUD, GPS, INS (Inertial Navigation System), and TCAS as well as PMP (a propulsion modification to improve low-altitude engine thrust). Many USAF variants (T-38A and AT-38B) are being converted to the T-38C standard.

The fighter version of the N-156 was eventually selected for the US Military Assistance Program and produced as the F-5 Freedom Fighter. Many of these have since reverted to a weapons training role as various air forces have introduced newer types into service. The F-5G was an advanced single engine variant later renamed the F-20 Tigershark.

Operational history

The USAF Strategic Air Command (SAC) had T-38 Talons in service from 1978 until SAC's deactivation in 1991.These aircraft were used to enhance the career development of bomber co-pilots through the "Accelerated Copilot Enrichment Program." They were later used as proficiency aircraft for all B-52 and B-1 pilots, as well as Lockheed SR-71, U-2, Boeing KC-135, and KC-10 pilots. SAC's successor, the Air Combat Command (ACC), continues to retain T-38s as proficiency aircraft for U-2 pilots.

The Air Training Command's (ATC) successor, the Air Education and Training Command (AETC), uses the T-38C to prepare pilots for aircraft such as the F-15C Eagle and F-15E Strike Eagle, as well as the F-16 Fighting Falcon, B-52 Stratofortress, B-1B Lancer, A-10 Thunderbolt and F-22 Raptor. The AETC received T-38Cs in 2001 as part of the Avionics Upgrade Program.

The T-38Cs owned by the AETC have undergone propulsion modernization which replaces major engine components to enhance reliability and maintainability, and an engine inlet/injector modification to increase available takeoff thrust. These upgrades and modifications, with the Pacer Classic program, should extend the service life of T-38s past 2020.

Besides the USAF, USN and NASA, other T-38 operators include the German Air Force (Luftwaffe), the Portuguese Air Force, the Republic of China Air Force, and the Turkish Air Force.

RQ-5 Hunter

The RQ-5 Hunter unmanned aerial vehicle (UAV) was originally intended to serve as the United States Army's Short Range UAV system for division and corps commanders.

It took off and landed (using arresting gear) on runways.

It used a gimbaled EO/IR sensor to relay its video in real time via a second airborne Hunter over a C-band line-of-sight data link.

The RQ-5 is based on the Hunter UAV that was developed by Israel Aircraft Industries.

The RQ-5 is based on the Hunter UAV

Hunter deployed in 1999 to Kosovo to support NATO operations. Although production was cancelled in 1996, seven low rate initial production (LRIP) systems of eight aircraft each were acquired, four of which remained in service: one for training and three for doctrine development and exercise and contingency support. Hunter was to be replaced by the RQ-7 Shadow, but instead of being replaced, the Army's has kept both systems in operation, because the Hunter has significantly large payload, range, and time-on-station capabilities than the Shadow.

Significant operation success in Kosovo led to resumption of production and technical improvements, and the system is at present in operational use in Iraq and other military operations. The system has also been armed with the Viper Strike munition.

The Army's Unmanned Aircraft Systems Training Battalion at Fort Huachuca, AZ trains soldiers and civilians in the operation and maintenance of the Hunter UAV.

In 2004, the United States Department of Homeland Security, Bureau of Customs and Border Protection, Office of Air and Marine utilized the Hunter under a trial program for border patrol duties.

During this program, the Hunter flew 329 flight hours, resulting in 556 detections.

A version armed with the Northrop Grumman GBU-44/B Viper Strike weapon system is known as the MQ-5A/B.

Grumman C-2 Greyhound

The Grumman C-2 Greyhound is a twin-engine, high-wing cargo aircraft, designed to carry supplies and mail to and from aircraft carriers of the United States Navy.

Its primary mission is carrier onboard delivery (COD).

The aircraft provides critical logistics support to carrier strike groups.

The aircraft is mainly used to transport high-priority cargo, mail and passengers between carriers and shore bases, and can deliver items like jet engines, and special stores.

Prototypes C-2s first flew in 1964 and production followed the next year.

The initial Greyhound aircraft were overhauled in 1973.

More C-2s were ordered in the 1980s. Further improvements to the C-2 have followed.

The C-2 Greyhound, a derivative of the E-2 Hawkeye, shares wings and power plants with the E-2 but has a widened fuselage with a rear loading ramp.

The first of two prototypes flew in 1964.

After successful testing, Grumman began production of the aircraft in 1965.

The C-2 replaced the piston-engined C-1 Trader in the COD role.

The original C-2A aircraft were overhauled to extend their operational life in 1973.

A C-2A in July 1988, based at Naval Air Station, Sigonella (Sicily, Italy)

Powered by two Allison T56 turboprop engines, the C-2A can deliver up to 10,000 pounds (4,500 kg) of cargo, passengers or both. It can also carry litter patients in medical evacuation missions. A cage system or transport stand restrains cargo during carrier launch and landing. The large aft cargo ramp and door and a powered winch allow straight-in rear cargo loading and unloading for fast turnaround. The Greyhound's ability to airdrop supplies and personnel, fold its wings, and generate power for engine starting and other uses provide an operational versatility found in no other cargo aircraft.

The aircraft has four vertical stabilizers because of aircraft carrier hangar deck height restrictions. Only three of these stabilizers have working rudders. For adequate directional control of an aircraft of this size, a single rudder would have been too tall. It also places the outboard rudder surfaces directly in line with the propeller wash, providing effective yaw control even as the plane's airspeed approaches zero, as during takeoff and landing.

In 1984, the Navy ordered 39 new C-2A aircraft to replace older airframes. Dubbed the Reprocured C-2A (C-2A(R)) due to the similarity to the original, the new aircraft has airframe improvements and better avionics. The older C-2As were phased out in 1987, and the last of the new models was delivered in 1990.

The 36 C-2A(R)s are undergoing a critical Service Life Extension Program (SLEP). The lifespan of the C-2A(R) was 10,000 hours, or 15,000 carrier landings; current plans require the C-2A to perform its mission supporting battle group operational readiness through 2015.

The landing limit is quickly approaching for most of the airframes, and the SLEP will increase the Greyhound's projected life to 15,000 hours or 36,000 landings.

Once the program is complete, it will allow the current 36 aircraft to operate until 2027.

The SLEP includes structural improvements to the center wing, navigational upgrades including the addition of GPS and the dual CAINS II Navigation System, the addition of crash survivable flight incident recorders, and a Ground Proximity Warning System.

The first upgraded C-2A(R) left NAVAIR Depot North Island on 12 September 2005, after sitting on the ground for three and a half years while the SLEP was developed and installed.

A second airframe is currently nearing completion and it is anticipated that the remaining 34 aircraft will all undergo the SLEP upgrade within the next five years as operations and schedule permit.

The eight-bladed NP2000 propeller is another part of this upgrade and is expected to be installed by 2010.

In November 2008, the company also obtained a $37m contract for the maintenance, logistics and aviation administration services over five years for the

C-2A fleet assigned to VX-20 test and evaluation squadron at Patuxent River. Northrop Grumman is currently working on an upgraded C-2 version.

A C-2A taxis prior to takeoff on a flight to USS John F. Kennedy (CV-67) in Feb 1984. This was the first Greyhound delivered in 1966.

Between November 1985 and February 1987, VR-24 (the former Navy Transport Squadron) and its seven reprocured C-2As demonstrated the aircraft's exceptional operational readiness.

The squadron delivered 2,000,000 pounds (910 t) of cargo, 2,000,000 pounds (910 t) of mail and 14,000 passengers in the European and Mediterranean theatres.

The C-2A(R) also served the carrier battle groups during Operations Desert Shield and Desert Storm, as well as currently during Operation Enduring Freedom.

The Common Support Aircraft was once considered as a replacement for the C-2, but failed to materialize.

Currently, there are no plans to replace the C-2A(R) fleet, and there are no replacement aircraft in development.

Interior view from the tail of a C-2A Greyhound assigned to Fleet Logistics Support Squadron 40 (VRC-40)

The USN was exploring a replacement for the C-2, including the V-22 Osprey as of September 2009.

Northrop Grumman E-2 Hawkeye

The Grumman E-2 Hawkeye is an American all-weather, aircraft carrier-capable tactical airborne early warning (AEW) aircraft.

This twin-turboprop aircraft was designed and developed during the late 1950s and early 1960s by the Grumman Aircraft Company for the United States Navy as a replacement for the earlier E-1 Tracer, which was rapidly becoming obsolete.

The aircraft's performance has been upgraded with the E-2B, and E-2C versions, where most of the changes were made to the radar and radio communications due to advances in electronic integrated circuits and other electronics. The fourth version of the Hawkeye is the E-2D, which first flew in 2007.

The E-2 also received the nickname "Super Fudd" because it replaced the E-1 Tracer "Willy Fudd". In recent decades, the E-2 has been commonly referred to as the "Hummer" because of the distinctive sounds of its turboprop engines, quite unlike that of turbojet and turbofan jet engines.

The E-2 and its sister, the C-2 Greyhound, are currently the only propeller airplanes that operate from aircraft carriers. In addition to U.S. Navy service, smaller numbers of E-2s have been sold to the armed forces of Egypt, France, Israel, Japan, Mexico, Singapore and Taiwan.

Two US Navy E-2C Hawkeye flying by Mount Fuji, Japan

Continual improvements in airborne radars through 1956 led to the construction of AEW airplanes by several different countries and several different armed forces.

The functions of command and control and sea & air surveillance were also added. The first carrier-based aircraft to perform these missions for the U.S. Navy and its allies was the Douglas AD Skyraider, which was replaced in US Navy service by the Grumman E-1 Tracer, which was a modified version of the S-2 Tracker twin-engine anti-submarine warfare aircraft, where the radar was carried in an aerofoil-shaped radome carried above the aircraft's fuselage.

The E-1 was used by the U.S. Navy from 1958 to 1977.

In 1956, the U.S. Navy developed a requirement for an airborne early warning aircraft where its data could be integrated into the Naval Tactical Data System aboard the Navy's ships, with a design from Grumman being selected to meet this requirement in March 1957.

Its design, initially designated W2F-1, but later redesignated the E-2A Hawkeye, was the first carrier plane that had been designed from its wheels up as an AEW and command and control airplane.

The problems facing the design engineers at Grumman were immense and were compounded by having to constrain the design to enable the aircraft to operate from the older 'modified Essex class aircraft carriers'. These 'smaller' carriers were built during WW2 and later modified to allow them to operate jet aircraft. Consequently, various height, weight and length restrictions had to be factored into the E-2A design, resulting in some handling characteristics which were less than ideal.

The E-2A only operated from the modified Essex class for a few years before the ships were decommissioned, and it's likely the design would have benefited considerably if this requirement had never been imposed.

The first prototype, acting as an aerodynamic testbed only, flew on 21 October 1960, with the first fully equipped aircraft following on 19 April 1961. The E-2A entered U.S. Navy service on January 1964.

Ripples appear along the fuselage of a US Navy E-2C due to loads from landing on the USS Harry S. Truman (CVN-75)

By 1965 the major development problems delaying the E-2A Hawkeye got so bad that the aircraft was actually cancelled after 59 aircraft had already been built. Particular difficulties were being experienced due to inadequate cooling in the closely packed avionics compartment. Early computer and complex avionics systems generated considerable heat; without proper ventilation this would lead to system failures.

These failures continued long after the aircraft entered service and at one point reliability was so bad the entire fleet of aircraft was grounded. The airframe was also prone to corrosion, a serious problem in a carrier based aircraft.

After Navy officials had been forced to explain to Congress why four production contracts had been signed before avionics testing had been completed, action was taken; Grumman and the US Navy scrambled to improve the design. The unreliable rotary drum computer was replaced by a Litton L-304 digital computer and various avionic systems were replaced – the upgraded aircraft were designated E-2Bs. In total, 49 of the 59 E-2As were upgraded to E-2B standard.

These aircraft replaced the E-1B Tracers in the various US Navy AEW squadrons and it was the E-2B that was to set a new standard for carrier based AEW aircraft.

Although the upgraded E-2B was a vast improvement on the unreliable E-2A, it was an interim measure. The US Navy knew the design had much greater capability and had yet to achieve the performance and reliability parameters set out in the original 1957 design. In April 1968 a reliability improvement program was instigated. In addition, now that the capabilities of the aircraft were starting to be realized, more were desired; 28 new E-2Cs were ordered to augment the 49 E-2Bs that would be upgraded. Improvements in the new and upgraded aircraft were concentrated in the radar and computer performance.

Two E-2A test machines were modified as prototypes of the E-2C, with the first flying on 20 January 1971. Trials proved satisfactory and the E-2C was ordered into production, with the first production machine performing its initial flight on 23 September 1972. The original E-2C, known as Group 0, consisted of 55 aircraft with the first aircraft becoming operational in 1973. They began arriving on carriers in the 1980s, serving until the 1990s when they were replaced by Group II aircraft in first-line service. Some ended up in the US Navy Reserve, being used to track drug smugglers.

After the experience with the E-2A/B, the E-2C Group 0 was an outstanding aircraft in operation and provided an effective partner to Grumman F-14 Tomcat fighters; monitoring the airspace and then vectoring Tomcats over the Link-4 datalink to destroy potential threat with long range Phoenix air-to-air missiles.

The next production run, between 1988 and 1991, saw 18 aircraft built to the Group I standard. Group I aircraft replaced the

E-2's older APS-125 radar and T56-A-425 turboprops with their improvements; the APS-139 radar system and T56-A-427 turboprops. The first Group I aircraft entered service on August 1981. Upgrading the Group 0 aircraft to Group 1 specifications was considered, but the cost was comparable to a new production aircraft, so upgrades were not conducted. Group 1 aircraft were only flown by the Atlantic fleet squadrons. This version of the E-2 was followed within a few years by the more-improved Group II, which had the improved APS-145 radar. Group II aircraft have been incrementally upgraded with new navigation systems, better situational display, and computerized electronics; culminating in the E-2C Hawkeye 2000 variant (sometimes called the Group III). A total of 50 Group II aircraft were delivered, 12 being upgraded Group I aircraft. This new version entered service in June 1992 and served with the Pacific and Atlantic Fleet squadrons.

By 1997 the US Navy intended that all the front line squadrons would be equipped, for a total of 75 Group II aircraft. However Grumman merged with Northrop in 1994 and plans began on the next upgrade, known as the Group II Plus, which eventually became known as the Hawkeye 2000. The Hawkeye 2000 featured the APS-145 radar with a new mission computer and CIC (Combat Information Center) workstations (Advanced Control Indicator Set or ACIS), and carries the

U.S. Navy's new CEC (cooperative engagement capability) data-link system. It is also fitted with a larger capacity vapor cycle avionics cooling system. A variant of the Group II with the upgrades to the mission computer and CIC workstations is referred to as the MCU/ACIS. All Group II aircraft have had their 1960s vintage computer-processors replaced by a mission computer with the same functionality but built using more modern computer technology. This is referred to as the GrIIM RePr (Group II Mission Computer Replacement Program, pronounced "grim reaper").

Starting in 2007 a hardware and software upgrade package began to be added to existing Hawkeye 2000 aircraft. This upgrade allows faster processing, double current trackfile capacity and access to satellite information networks. Hawkeye 2000 cockpits being upgraded include solid-state glass displays, modern weather detection systems and a GPS-approach capability.

E-2D Advanced Hawkeye

Though once considered for replacement by the "Common Support Aircraft", this conception never went into production, and the Hawkeye will continue in its role as the Navy's primary AEW aircraft for years into the future in the E-2D version.

The latest version of the E-2, the E-2D Advanced Hawkeye, is currently under development and the first two aircraft, "Delta One" and "Delta Two" remain in flight testing and several other aircraft are currently undergoing Initial Operational Test and Evaluation with Test and Evaluation Squadron One at [NAS Patuxent River].

The E-2D features an entirely new avionics suite, including the new APY-9 radar, radio suite, mission computer, integrated satellite communications capability, flight management system, improved T56-A-427A turboprop engines, a new tactical glass cockpit and the potential capability for air-to-air refueling.

The APY-9 radar features an Active Electronically Scanned Array, which adds electronic scanning to the mechanical rotation of the radar in its radome.

The E-2D will include provisions for either one of the pilots to act as a Tactical 4th Operator, who will have access to the full range of the mission's acquired data.

The E-2D's first flight occurred on 3 August 2007. On May 8, 2009, an E-2D Advanced Hawkeye used its Cooperative Engagement Capability system to engage an overland cruise missile with a Standard Missile SM-6 fired from another platform in an integrated fire-control system test. Deliveries of initial production E-2Ds to Navy began in 2010.

On 4 February 2010, Delta One conducted the first E-2D carrier landing aboard the USS Harry S. Truman as a part of carrier suitability testing. On 27 September 2011, an E-2D was successfully launched by the prototype Electromagnetic Aircraft Launch System (EMALS) at Naval Air Engineering Station Lakehurst.

The first two E-2D prototypes

The E-2 is a high-wing airplane, with one turboprop engine in each wing, and retractable tricycle landing gear. As with most carrier-borne airplanes, the E-2 is equipped with a tail hook for landings, and it is capable of using the aircraft carrier's catapults for takeoff. A distinguishing feature of the Hawkeye is its 24-foot (7.3 m) diameter rotating dome that is mounted above its fuselage and wings.

This carries the E-2's primary antennas for its long-range radar and IFF systems. No other carrier-borne aircraft possesses one of these, and among land-based aircraft, they are mostly seen atop the Boeing E-3 Sentry, a larger AWACS airplane operated by the U.S. Air Force and NATO air forces in large numbers.

The aircraft is operated by a crew of five, with the pilot and co-pilot on the flight deck and the combat information center officer, air control officer and radar operator stations located in the rear fuselage directly beneath the rotodome.

In U.S. service, the E-2 Hawkeye provides all-weather airborne early warning and command and control capabilities for all aircraft-carrier battle groups. In addition, its other purposes include sea and land surveillance, the control of the aircraft carrier's fighter planes for air defense, the control of strike aircraft on offensive missions, the control of search and rescue missions for naval aviators and sailors lost at sea, and for the relay of radio communications, air-to-air and ship-to-air. It can also serve in an air traffic control capacity in emergency situations when land-based ATC is unavailable.

The E-2C and E-2D Hawkeyes use advanced electronic sensors combined with digital computerized signal processing, especially its radars, for early warning of enemy aircraft attacks and anti-ship missile attacks, and the control of the carrier's combat air patrol (CAP) fighters, and secondarily for surveillance of the surrounding sea and land for enemy warships and guided-missile launchers, and any other electronic surveillance missions as directed.

Operational history

The E-2A entered U.S. Navy service on January 1964, and in April 1964 with VAW-11 at NAS North Island. The first deployment was aboard the USS Kitty Hawk (CVA-63) during 1965.

Since entering combat during the Vietnam War, the E-2 has served the US Navy around the world, acting as the electronic "eyes of the fleet". Hawkeyes from the air wing VAW-123 aboard the aircraft carrier USS America (CV-66) directed a group of F-14 Tomcat fighters flying the Combat Air Patrol during Operation El Dorado Canyon, the joint strike of two Carrier Battle Groups in the Mediterranean Sea against Libyan terrorist targets during 1986. More recently, E-2Cs provided the command and control for both aerial warfare and land-attack missions during the Persian Gulf War.

Hawkeyes have supported the U.S. Coast Guard, the U.S. Customs Service, and American federal and state police forces during anti-drug operations.

In the mid-1980s, several E-2Cs were borrowed from the U.S. Navy and given to the U.S. Coast Guard and the U.S. Customs Service for counternarcotics (CN) and maritime interdiction operations (MIO).

A US Navy E-2C of VAW-117 approaches to land on the flight deck of the USS John C. Stennis (CVN-74), clearly showing the new eight-bladed propellers installed on all of the Navy's E-2Cs

This also led to the Coast Guard building a small cadre of Naval Flight Officers (NFOs), starting with the recruitment and interservice transfer of Navy flight officers with E-2 flight experience and the flight training of other junior Coast Guard officers as NFOs.

A fatal aircraft mishap on 24 August 1990 involving a Coast Guard E-2C at the former Naval Station Roosevelt Roads in Puerto Rico prompted the Coast Guard to discontinue flying E-2Cs and to return its E-2Cs to the Navy.

The U.S Customs Service also returned its E-2Cs to the Navy and concentrated on the use of former U.S. Navy P-3 Orion aircraft in the CN role.

E-2C Hawkeye squadrons played a critical role in air operations during Operation Desert Storm. In one instance, a Hawkeye crew provided critical air control direction to two F/A-18 Hornet aircrew, resulting in the shootdown of two Iraqi MiG-21s.

During Operations Southern Watch and Desert Fox, Hawkeye crews continued to provide thousands of hours of air coverage, while providing air-to-air and air-to-ground command and control in a number of combat missions.

The E-2 Hawkeye is a crucial component of all U.S. Navy carrier air wings, and each carrier is equipped with four Hawkeyes (five in some situations), allowing for continuous 24-hour-a-day operation of at least one Hawkeye, and allowing for one or two of them to be undergoing maintenance in the aircraft carrier's hangar deck at all times. Until 2005 the US Navy Hawkeye's were organised into East and West coast wings, supporting the respective fleets. However, the East coast wing was disestablished and all aircraft are now organised into a single wing based at Point Mugu, California. Six E-2C Hawkeye aircraft are deployed by the US Naval Reserve for drug interdiction and homeland security operations.

During Operation Enduring Freedom and Operation Iraqi Freedom all ten Regular Navy Hawkeye squadrons flew overland sorties. They provided battle management for attack of enemy ground targets, close-air-support coordination, combat search and rescue control, airspace management, as well as datalink and communication relay for both land and naval forces.

During the aftermath of Hurricane Katrina, three Hawkeye squadrons (two Regular Navy and one Navy Reserve) were deployed in support of civilian relief efforts including Air Traffic Control responsibilities spanning three states, and the control of U.S. Army, U.S. Navy, U.S. Air Force, U.S. Marine Corps, U.S. Coast Guard, and Army National Guard and Air National Guard helicopter rescue units.

Hawkeye 2000s first deployed in 2003 aboard USS Nimitz (CVN-68) with VAW-117, the "Wallbangers", and CVW-11. U.S. Navy E-

2C Hawkeyes have been upgraded with eight-bladed propellers as part of the NP2000 program; the first squadron to cruise with the new propellers was VAW-124 "Bear Aces".

The Hawkeye 2000 version can track more than 2,000 targets simultaneously (while at the same time, detecting 20,000 simultaneously) to a range greater than 400 mi (640 km) and simultaneously guide 40–100 air to air intercepts or air to surface engagements. VAW-120, the E-2C fleet replacement squadron began receiving E-2D Advanced Hawkeyes for training use in July 2010. Initial operating capability for an E-2D fleet squadron ready for operational deployment has slipped to October 2014.

An E-2C Hawkeye

Northrop Grumman EA-6B Prowler

The Northrop Grumman (formerly Grumman) EA-6B Prowler is a twin-engine, mid-wing electronic warfare aircraft modified from the basic A-6 Intruder airframe.

The EA-6B has been in service with the U.S. Armed Forces from 1971 through the present, during which it has carried out numerous missions for jamming enemy radar systems, and in gathering radio intelligence on those and other enemy air defense systems. In addition, the EA-6B is capable of carrying and firing anti-radiation missiles (ARM), such as the HARM missile.

The aircrew of the EA-6B consists of one pilot and three Electronic Countermeasures Officers, though it is not uncommon for only 2 ECMOs to be used on missions.

From the 1998 retirement of the United States Air Force EF-111 Raven electronic warfare aircraft, the EA-6B was the only dedicated electronic warfare plane available for missions by the U.S. Navy, the U.S. Marine Corps, and the U.S. Air Force until the fielding of the Navy's EA-18G Growler in 2009.

The EA-6A "Electric Intruder" was developed for the U.S. Marine Corps during the 1960s to replace its EF-10B Skyknights.

The EA-6A was a direct conversion of the standard A-6 Intruder airframe, with two seats, equipped with electronic warfare (EW) equipment.

The EA-6A was used by three Marine Corps squadrons during the War in Vietnam. A total of 27 EA-6As were produced, with 15 of these being newly-manufactured ones. Most of these EA-6As were retired from service in the 1970s with the last few being retired in the 1980s. The EA-6A was essentially an interim warplane until the more-advanced EA-6B could be designed and built.

A U.S. Navy EA-6B Prowler

The substantially redesigned and more advanced EA-6B was developed beginning in

1966 as a replacement for EKA-3B Skywarriors for the U.S. Navy.

The forward fuselage was lengthened to create a rear area for a larger four-seat cockpit, and an antenna fairing was added to the tip of its vertical stabilizer.

The Prowler first flew on 25 May 1968, and it entered service on aircraft carriers in July 1971. Three prototype EA-6Bs were converted from A-6As, and five EA-6Bs were developmental airplanes. A total of 170 EA-6B production aircraft were manufactured from 1966 through 1991.

The EA-6B Prowler is powered by two turbojet engines, and it is capable of high subsonic speeds. Due to its extensive electronic warfare operations, and the aircraft's age (produced until 1991), the EA-6B is a high-maintenance aircraft, and it also has undergone more frequent equipment upgrades than any other aircraft in the Navy or Marine Corps.

Although designed as an electronic warfare and command-and-control aircraft for air strike missions, the EA-6B is also capable of attacking some surface targets on its own, in particular enemy radar sites and surface-to-air missile launchers. In addition, the EA-6B is capable of gathering electronic signals intelligence.

The EA-6B Prowler has been continually upgraded over the years.

BQM-74 Chukar

The BQM-74 Chukar is a series of aerial target drones produced by Northrop. The Chukar has gone through three major revisions, including the initial MQM-74A Chukar I, the MQM-74C Chukar II, and the BQM-74C Chukar III. They are recoverable, remote controlled, subsonic aerial target, capable of speeds up to Mach 0.86 and altitudes from 30 to 40,000 ft (10 to 12,000 m).

BQM-74 Chukar

The BQM-74E is propelled during flight by a single Williams J400 (J400-WR-404) turbojet engine, which produces a maximum thrust of 240 pounds force (1068 N) at sea level. The BQM-74 is launched from a zero length ground launcher utilizing dual Jet Assisted Takeoff (JATO) bottles. When equipped with an air launch kit, the BQM-74 can be air launched from a TA-4J, F-16, Grumman Gulfstream I or DC-130 aircraft. The BQM-74 is used primarily as a realistic aerial target, capable of simulating enemy threats for gunnery and missile training exercises.

Drones are capable of being recovered following a training exercise. A parachute is deployed by remote control or if the remote control link is severed and a flotation kit can be added for sea-based recovery. If recovery of the drone is required, special telemetry warheads are used on the defensive missile in place of explosives.

This telemetry warhead is desirable since it allows for extensive analysis of the performance of the defensive missile, including miss distance information that determines if a real warhead would have damaged the target. A direct hit would likely destroy the drone. Gunnery systems would use non-explosive dummy munitions. Since gunnery systems are aimed in front of a moving target so it will fly through the blast-fragments, dummy munitions do not have to directly hit a target. Analysis of radar data would determine if the dummy munitions would have damaged the target drone.

Viper Strike

Northrop Grumman announces an unspecified additional contract to deliver "multiple" GBU-44 Viper Strikes beginning to the Joint Attack Munition Systems (JAMS) Project Office at Redstone Arsenal, AL, beginning in 2011, for eventual integration onto the KC-130J Harvest Hawk

Industrial partners may change, in the wake of MBDA's December 2011 acquisition. Elbit Systems of America currently manufactures some of the guidance equipment, but MBDA may wish to move that in-house.

Unless otherwise specified, contracts are awarded by the U.S. Army Aviation and Missile Command in Redstone Arsenal, AL, USA.

Sept 9/12: Cessna test. MBDA announces that its GBU-44/E Viper Strike successfully hit eight vehicles travelling at extremely high speeds in varying realistic scenarios, after being dropped from a Cessna 208B Caravan test aircraft at White Sands Missile Range, NM.

The chosen platform is as important as the results. Iraq has already created AC-208 Combat Caravans that fire more expensive Hellfire missiles, and the ability to arm small planes like the Caravan adds a whole new dimension to Viper Strike's potential usefulness, and widens its potential customer base.

April 16/12: KC-130J test. MBDA announces that its GBU-44/E Viper Strike scored "multiple direct hits", after being launched from the KC-130J Harvest HAWK's new "Derringer Door" during developmental testing at China Lake, CA. Viper Strike also proved out its new fast attack software load, designed to improve performance against time sensitive targets.

Jan 17/12: A $6.9 million firm-fixed-price contract modification for "Viper rounds, parts and engineering services." MBDA is now the contractor, though the announcement hews to the name in the contract, which is Northrop Grumman Systems Corp. in Huntsville, AL.

Work will be performed by MBDA in Huntsville, Ala., with an estimated completion date of Aug 31/12. One bid was solicited, with one bid received (W31P4Q-07-C-0268).

Dec 12/11: European missile giant MBDA announces that it has bought Northrop Grumman's Huntsville, AL Viper Strike facility, and the weapon.

MBDA sees it as a proven option for armed UAVs, to complement products like their LMM mini-missile, which is currently in development. Viper Strike's ability to arm transport aircraft, helicopters, and other platforms may also offer an opportunity for MBDA. After tallying their expenses over Libya, European militaries may well look to European firms for precision weapons and deployment systems, that cost less than the standard solution of high-end fighters dropping laser-guided bombs. MBDA.

Bought by MBDA

Aug 22/11: Northrop Grumman announces an unspecified additional contract to deliver "multiple" GBU-44 Viper Strikes beginning to the Joint Attack Munition Systems (JAMS) Project Office at Redstone Arsenal, AL, beginning in 2011, for eventual integration onto the KC-130J Harvest Hawk. See also June 2/10 entry.

All the Viper Strike munitions on Harvest Hawk will now carry the latest software load, which greatly enhances the weapon's effectiveness against moving targets. In recent testing at China Lake, CA, Viper Strike scored multiple hits against moving vehicles in various scenarios.

Aug 19/11: Aviation Week reports on 2 key milestones for the program. One is the addition of the MQ-8C/ Fire-X. The other is weapons approval for the MQ-8B, beginning with the APKWS-II laser-guided 70mm rocket that's already cleared for use from Navy ships. Raytheon's laser-guided short-range Griffin mini-missile is slated for a demonstration before the end of August 2011, and will be the platform's next weapon, as opposed to Northrop Grumman's own GBU-44 Viper Strike.

June 2/10: Northrop Grumman announces a contract, to deliver 65 Viper Strike munitions to the Joint Attack Munition Systems (JAMS) Project Office, within the Program Executive Office Missiles and Space at Redstone Arsenal, AL. The Viper Strikes will be delivered in 2010, for eventual integration onto the KC-130J Harvest Hawk platform.

April 10/10: The KC-130J Harvest Hawk roll-on/roll-off gunship kit completes

Phase 1 testing at Pax River, MD, and leaves for required maintenance and continued testing at NAVAIR's China Lake, CA range. NAVAIR now says that it is working a complimentary effort to test and deploy the Standoff Precision Guided Munition (SOPGM, aka. "Viper Strike") as a stand alone capability for Harvest HAWK's initial fielding, and that the first aircraft is scheduled to deploy by summer 2010 equipped with the AN/AQS-30 TSS, Hellfire missiles, and SOPGM. NAVAIR release.

FY 2005 – 2009

Sept 1/09: Northrop Grumman announces that its MQ-5B Hunter UAV has successfully completed testing of the new GPS-guided Viper Strike (GPS VS) at White Sands Missile Range, NM, and that these weapons "will soon deploy to theater on board Hunter in support of contingency operations."

The announcement is a breakthrough for the Viper Strike, on two fronts. One front is the addition of GPS-based guidance. The other is the fact that Viper Strike had not been deployed to the front lines due to inter-service disagreements, and does not appear to have been been brought to fruition on US Special Operations Command's AC-130s either. See also StrategyPage.

April 2/09: Northrop Grumman Systems Corp. in Huntsville, AL won an $11.3 million firm-fixed-price contract with cost plus fixed fee, line items contract for Viper Strike Munitions and engineering services. Work is to be performed at Huntsville, AL, with an estimated completion date of April 30/10. One bid was solicited and one bid received (W31P4Q-07-C-0268).

The Viper Strike program has been restructured, consolidating the laser-guided Direct Attack and the new GPS-guided variant into a single version, and changing the Army's order totals. Instead of 137 Direct Attack munitions, The US Army is ordering 49 of the new GPS-enabled version, plus 15 additional direct attack kits, 3 Hunter integration kits, and MQ-5B Hunter integration, testing, and eventual fielding. US SOCOM is also switching its order to the new GPS-enabled version.

Sept 26/07: Northrop Grumman Systems Corp. in Huntsville, Ala. received a $16.1 million modification to a cost-plus-fixed-fee and firm-fixed-price contract for Viper Strike Munitions and engineering services. Work will be performed in Huntsville, AL and is expected to be complete by Dec 31/08. This was a sole source contract initiated on Sept. 5, 2007 (W31P4Q-07-C-0268).

March 12/07: AC-130. Northrop Grumman of Linthcum, MD received a $7.4 million contract modification for the demonstration of their Viper Strike munition on the AC-130 gunship as a ranged precision-guided munition. This modification action adds the requirement for the contractor to support an extended user evaluation of the munitions on the AC-130, and brings the current total maximum estimated cost of this contract to $29.4 million (H92222-05-C-0020, Modification P00012).

Work will be performed out of Huntsville, AL, and is incrementally funded based on performance. The initial proof of concept work is to be complete by October 2007.

Feb. 28/07: Northrop Grumman announces that a successful round of RQ-5A Hunter and Viper Strike testing was conducted at White Sands Missile Range, NM in January 2007 against moving and stationary targets. The weapons tests were conducted under the auspices of the U.S. Army's Program Executive Office (PEO) for Aviation and the PEO for Missiles and Space.

Aug 4/05: Northrop Grumman of Linthcum, MD received a sole-source $22 million cost-plus incentive-fee Advanced Concept of Technology Demonstration contract (H92222-05-C-0020) for the demonstration of their Viper Strike munition as a Stand-off Precision Guided Munition on the AC-130 Specter gunship.

Work on this contract will be performed out of Huntsville, AL and is being incrementally funded based on performance. The initial increment of work was expected to be complete in December 2005, and all Initial Proof of Concept work was expected to be complete by December 2006. The $22-million contract is an Advanced Concept Technology Demonstration program with a potential full value of $48.6 million.

Bibliography

[1] "Elected Officers". Retrieved January 8, 2010.

[2] a b c d e f [investor.northropgrumman.com "NorthropGrumman_10k_20120208"]. NorthropGrumman.

[3] "SIPRI Top 100 Defence Contractors". Stockholm International Peace Research Institute.

[4] "Northrop Grumman Rises 10 Spots on DiversityInc's 2011 Top 50 Companies for Diversity List (NYSE:NOC)". Irconnect.com. March 10, 2011. Retrieved July 25, 2012.

[5] "Annual Income Statement". Retrieved March 13, 2008.

[6] "Fortune 500 2011". CNN.

[7] "Northrop Grumman Ranks in the Top Ten Military Friendly Employers (NYSE:NOC)". Irconnect.com. December 21, 2010. Retrieved July 25, 2012.

[8] "Northrop Grumman Announces Key Leadership and Organizational Changes". Northrop Grumman, January 14, 2008.

[9] Jacobs, Karen. "Northrop completes spin-off of ship business." Reuters, March 31, 2011.

[10] "Northrop Grumman Hopes for Big Role in DoD Bomber Plan[dead link]." Christie, R. The Wall Street Journal. July 10, 2006.

[11] "Northrop Grumman KC-30 marketing web site". Northrop Grumman. Archived from the original on February 12, 2007. Retrieved February 16, 2007.

[12] This story was written by 070107. ""Air Force Posts KC-X Request for Proposals", USAF news release, 2007-01-30". Af.mil. Retrieved July 25, 2012.

[13] EADS Shares Surge on $35B US Contract.

[14] Ostrower, Jon. "Northrop Grumman declines to bid on latest KC-X RFP". Flight International, March 9, 2010.

[15] "NASA Selects Companies for Heavy-Lift Vehicle Studies". NASA. Retrieved November 8, 2010.

[16] NG, DHS Technologies to support SICPS/TMSS United Press International.

[17] "$48 Million To Train Iraqi Army". Defense News. July 7, 2003.

[18] McDougall, Paul (November 15, 2005). "Virginia Taps Northrop Grumman for $2 Billion IT Overhaul". Information Week. Retrieved April 4, 2006.

[19] "Britain Issues $1.2B E-3D AWACS Support Contract". Defense Industry Daily. August 16, 2005. Retrieved April 4, 2006.

[20] Jourdan, Max (December 14, 2004). "Protecting people or profit?". BBC News. Retrieved April 4, 2006.

[21] Quintanilla, Jacob (June 29, 2004). "The "Invisible" U.S. War in Colombia". Resource Center of the Americas. Archived from the original on January 3, 2006. Retrieved April 5, 2006.

[22] http://www.nn.northropgrumman.com/news/2007/061207.pdf

[23] Pike, John. "Global Security: Mergers". Retrieved April 5, 2006.

[24] "Northrop Grumman Buys Builder of SpaceShipOne". SPACE.com. July 20, 2007. Retrieved July 25, 2012.

[25] "Northrop Grumman's National Work Force Center Initiative". Retrieved April 22, 2009.

[26] "Rapid City". Keloland.com. December 6, 2011. Retrieved July 25, 2012.

[27] "Northrop Grumman Statement to News Media Regarding the Release of Our Employees in Colombia". Irconnect.com. July 3, 2008. Retrieved July 25, 2012.

[28] Northrop Grumman: About Us. Northrop Grumman, Retrieved June 23, 2010.

[29] a b Lubove, Seth (January 6, 2003). "Company of the Year: Northrop—We See

You, Saddam". Forbes Magazine. Retrieved August 24, 2011.

[30] "Northrop's Sugar to Retire; Wesley Bush Named Chief (Update2)". Bloomberg. September 16, 2009.

[31] a b "Northrop Grumman Selects Falls Church Location for New Corporate Office (NYSE:NOC)." Northrop Grumman. July 12, 2010. Retrieved on September 6, 2011. "[...]2980 Fairview Park Drive, Falls Church, Va.[...]"

[32] "Jefferson CDP, Virginia." U.S. Census Bureau. Retrieved on September 6, 2011.

[33] "Company Locations." Northrop Grumman. Retrieved on September 6, 2011. "Northrop Grumman Corporation 2980 Fairview Park Drive Falls Church, VA 22042".

[34] Hyland, Alexa. "SoCal's Aerospace Sector Still Has Lots of Lift[dead link]." Los Angeles Business Journal. January 11, 2010. Retrieved January 10, 2010.

[35] "Company Locations." Northrop Grumman. Retrieved May 12, 2009.

[36] "The Ticker." Washington Post, January 4, 2010. Retrieved on January 4, 2010.

[37] a b Crowe, Deborah. "Northrop to Move Corporate Office to D.C.[dead link]." Los Angeles Business Journal. January 4, 2010. Retrieved January 10, 2010.

[38] Haynes, V. Dion. "D.C. area jurisdictions vie to become new home of Northrop Grumman headquarters." Washington Post. Monday January 11, 2010. Retrieved February 13, 2010.

[39] "Forbes Names Northrop Grumman Company of the Year". Forbes Magazine. December 19, 2002. Retrieved April 4, 2006.

[40] "America's Best Big Companies". Forbes Magazine. 2006. Retrieved April 4, 2006.

[41] Northrop Grumman (March 20, 2006). Northrop Grumman Becomes Co-pilot for NASA's Great Moonbuggy Race. Press release.

[42] Northrop Grumman (March 31, 2006). Northrop Grumman Makes $25,000 Donation to Boys and Girls Club of Annapolis and Anne Arundel County. Press release.

[43] "Northrop Grumman Employees Charity Organization". Reading to Kids. 2005. Retrieved April 4, 2006.

[44] "Environmental Protection Agency". Yosemite.epa.gov. June 19, 2003. Retrieved July 25, 2012.

[45] Northrop Grumman. CorpWatch.org.

[46] "Defense PAC Contributions". Opensecrets.org. June 4, 2007. Retrieved July 25, 2012.

[47] "Northrop PAC Contribution". Opensecrets.org. Retrieved July 25, 2012.

[48] US: Roche Bails Out for Top Army Job Amid Scandal. CorpWatch.org.

[49] Flynn, Michael (2004). "Northrop Grumman". Right Web Profiles. Retrieved April 4, 2006.

[50] Merle, Renae (August 9, 2003). "Northrop Settles Billing Case: Shipbuilding Unit Allegedly Overbilled U.S. by $72 Million". Washington Post. Retrieved April 4, 2006.

[51] "Northrop Grumman pays $111 million to settle qui tam case against recent acquisition, TRW" Phillips and Cohen Press Release, June 9, 2003.

[52] "Scientist blew whistle on faulty military satellite parts; Northrop Grumman pays $325 million to settle case". Phillips & Cohen LLP Press Release, April 2, 2009.

[53] Drew, Christopher. "Military Contractor Agrees To Pay $325 Million To Settle Whistle-Blower Lawsuit". New York Times, April 3, 2009, p. B4.

[54] Rosalind Helderman and Anita Kumar (September 2, 2010). "Computer crash has tech world watching". Washington Post: p. B1.

[55] Kumar, Anita (September 2, 2010). "McDonnell: Some data may be lost as a result of computer outage". Washington Post. Retrieved September 3, 2010.